SHORT CUTS

INTRODUCTIONS TO FILM STUDIES

OTHER TITLES IN THE SHORT CUTS SERIES

ACTION MOVIES

THE CINEMA OF STRIKING BACK

HARVEY O'BRIEN

WALLFLOWER

LONDON and NEW YORK

A Wallflower Press Book
Published by
Columbia University Press
Publishers Since 1893
New York • Chichester, West Sussex
cup.columbia.edu

1007046473

A complete CIP record is available from the Library of Congress

ISBN 978-0-231-16331-6 (pbk. : alk. paper)
ISBN 978-0-231-85022-3 (e-book)

Columbia University Press books are printed on permanent and durable acid-free paper.
This book is printed on paper with recycled content.

Printed in the United States of America

p 10 9 8 7 6 5 4 3 2 1

CONTENTS

ACKNOWLEDGEMENTS

I wish to thank Yoram Allon and Jodie Taylor at Wallflower Press for their astounding patience. This book has been a long time coming. I would also like to thank my beautiful wife Catherine, who sacrificed her holidays to make sure I finished it.

Dedicated to Kay, who loved Arnold Schwarzenegger movies

PREFACE

So, why didn't you talk about [insert favourite (a) film (b) performer (c) director (d) theme or (e) theory]?' I am anticipating this question in both casual and formal conversation upon the publication of this book, and my answer is fairly simple – this is an introduction. In writing it I have omitted many things, including elements I would love to spend whole books on. But you have to start somewhere, and I hope readers find here a useful primer on the action film in a scholarly context. I also hope it will help you to enjoy them more, because I do, and I wouldn't have written this book if I didn't.

Lock and Load.

INTRODUCTION

Taking Action

In *Last Action Hero* (1993) a schoolboy bored by a lesson on Shakespeare dreams about a Schwarzenegger *Hamlet*. A trailer runs inside his head. There is gunplay, skull-hurling and one-liners. Schwarzenegger intones 'To be or not to be' and lights a cigar. An explosion rips through Elsinore as he concludes 'Not to be.' Action cinema is not about hesitation: it is about *taking* action. It is a cinema of will: the attempt to change the world, transcending the moral limits of a society that has failed its heroes. The ubertext of the genre, *Rambo: First Blood Part II* (1985), makes this clear. In its pre-credits sequence Rambo responds to Commander Trautman's request to return to Vietnam to seek out prisoners of war with the question 'Sir, do we get to win this time?' Trautman replies: 'This time it's up to you.'

The cinema of action is a cinema of striking back – of restoration and reassurance. Action heroes do not seek out adventure, they respond to dire necessity. In *Speed* (1994) the bus must never slow down or it will explode. In *Crank* (2006) Chelios becomes the bus – he has been poisoned, and if he does not keep his adrenaline up he will die before he can find a cure or at least punish those responsible. Action movies are therefore also a cinema of crisis and *reaction* – of attempting to restore agency through force of will. Though action movies seem to project hypermasculine triumphalism and redemption through violence, they thus represent a profoundly anxious attitude. This is a cinema of trauma and post-traumatic stress, a cinema of threat and unease in which action heroes, severed as they always are from a morally justifiable framework such as legitimate warfare (the war movie), police procedure (the crime thriller) or the *realpolitik* of political revolution

1

(art-house agitprop), must fight to remain heroes. Indeed, they become heroic through the act *of* fighting. The climax of *The A-Team* (2010) turns on BA Baracus's abandonment of his policy of non-violence following a stint in prison in which he has found spiritual enlightenment. He is out-quoted by Hannibal Smith in a dialectical citation of Gandhi. To BA's quote 'Victory attained through violence is tantamount to defeat', Hannibal retorts 'It is better to be violent if there is violence in our hearts than to put on the cloak of non-violence to cover impotence.' After some moments of reflection, BA gets back in the fight, flying through the air on a motorbike then breaking a man's back with a wrestling move.

The action film is best understood as a fusion of form and content – a cinema *of* action. It represents the idea and the ethic of action through a form in which action, agitation and movement are paramount. This is a conception of action that makes sense in philosophic terms. It is a cinema Friedrich Nietzsche would have understood. There are two branches of philosophical thought on action, one focused on interior processes of decision (volitionism), the other on external roots and causes (teleology). Both are applicable in studying the action film. Philosopher Rowland Stout says that action 'is the transformation of the world in the light of reasons' (2005: 6). Agency, he tells us, is central – the degree to which motivation, intention and the capacity to affect transformation is embodied in acts of will.

Schopenhauer and Nietzsche both wrote about the will, though in different ways. For Schopenhauer, the body acts because it is a manifestation of the will – the word become flesh, so to speak. The act of the will and the action of the body do not relate as cause and effect, but are one and the same: 'will that has become representation' (1958: 100), as he puts it. Put crudely, he might be saying 'actions speak louder than words (or thoughts)', or, in this case 'actions are thoughts'. He argued that only by living in the present moment (to simplify the concept) does a person realise the 'will-to-live' and possess the capacity to act.

Nietzsche did not accept Schopenhauer's conception of will, or rather he sought to complicate it by making it more dynamic. For Nietzsche, enacting the will is a process – a struggle – a set of actions within action that means that any act of will is an act of command and obedience working against constraint and resistance. The human body is, in his words, 'a social structure composed of many souls' (2003: 49), that require mastery: accepting the constraints of the body through assuming command of it. In other words the 'will-to-power' is action *in* action – the body is not static, iconic and unitary – it is responsive, reactive and reflexive.

In this philosophic sense, the hero in the action movie is very much an agent of will: a paradoxical figure of both compulsion and command. The cause-and-effect tango around which *The Terminator* (1984) is structured is a clear example: the machine is programmed, but responsive and adaptive, which challenges Reese to prove his humanity by exceeding his human limitations. In doing so he inspires Sarah to do likewise and take command of her future.

The teleology of the action film is revealing in terms of the study of social cause and effect (why a character acts), but it is manifestly a cinema of volition (how they act). Action movies are full of action: of spectacle, of violence, of acts of will and contest that make up the bulk of what the audience sees. Eric Lichtenfeld concludes his book *Actions Speak Louder* with a useful summation: 'the well written, well-performed, well-crafted action movie offers its audience something more vital than excitement. It offers a sense that the characters are actually experiencing what the filmmakers stage' (2007: 344). What is key here is the sense that Lichtenfeld describes of action *in action*. The well-realised action film, he argues, allows the audience to perceive the components of action: the struggle to overcome obstacles, to enact motion and to embody the will involved in any given scene or even any given (moving) image. The action movie works best when it is acting, in action, active, in progress – when its heroes are being tested and when the audience can see and understand what they are being tested by.

Action heroes respond to mortal threats directed at their weaknesses, overcome obstacles of increasing difficulty, and finally face (and vanquish) their nemesis to transform the world for the better. Action movies are also clearly a classical narrative cinema in this sense, offering catharsis through resolution of the disruption to the status quo. They are also something of a self-fulfilling prophecy, what Slavoj Žižek brands 'false activity' where 'you think you are active, but your true position, as embodied in the fetish, is passive' (2010: 401); a cathartic but disempowering articulation of the mechanisms of the real exercise of power. It is this that makes action films so fascinating to analyse: the more vehemently they profess assurance, the more clearly they manifest unease.

Though they evidently indulge in fantasy and wish-fulfillment, this by no means implies that the philosophies espoused by the action film are

3

without consequence. This is particularly well illustrated by the cultural influence of *Rambo: First Blood Part II,* which spread very quickly in the mid-1980s and caused alarm among critical observers. *Time Magazine* reported just one month after the film's release that the US Army had begun using film posters outside recruitment offices. Reviewing the film in *Time,* Richard Schickel observed 'if the most basic rule of the action movie is that no dangerous live rounds should be expended in making it, it is equally true that it should avoid cheap and superficial reference to dangerous, live moral issues as well' (1985). He argues that what he terms a 'decent movie' would encourage its audience to share the anguish of the families of real-life MIAs, and not indulge in symbolic victory. Perhaps it would, but that would be a different kind of movie. In fact that would be *The Deer Hunter* (1978). The 1980s were politically and socially different, and the action movie, which emerged fully fledged in this era, was arguably one of the most prominent signs of the attitude that prevailed in the closing years of the Cold War.

Stephen Prince warns against excessively mapping the politics and culture of the Reagan era onto its cinema, but concedes that the 'clearest correlations' (2007: 12) are to be found in the action genre. As David Reynolds (2009) has observed, America's culture wars have always been fought in their times of greatest prosperity. The years of Reaganomics, with their spiraling deficit but outward indications of growth and affluence, were very much the platform for a cultural 'hot front'.

Paul Monaco (2001) also makes this point in the context of an analysis of the 1960s, noting that as the real-life revolution failed, cinema took up the mythological mantle of liberal conscience. As Christopher Sharrett has remarked, the cinema occupied a particular position throughout this era because it was 'so heavily involved in a new yet familiar American apocalypticism' (1993: 1) coinciding with the growth of postmodernism, and this contained a powerful element of reaction to the uncertain sociopolitical paradigms of the 1970s, particularly discourse around gender and race.

Susan Jeffords (1994) has examined this in the context of the image of the 'hard body'. She argues that the remasculinisation of America began with the reconstitution of Vietnam. This was closely integrated with repatriation through surrogate fathers in narratives dramatising the patrimony of the American nation, and, by natural extension, reasserting the patriarchy of the Presidency under Ronald Reagan and George H. W. Bush. This would reach

Embodying the Presidency: Harrison Ford fights back in *Air Force One* (1997)

something of a metaphoric apex much later in *Air Force One* (1997) where the hero *is* the President and he is also, significantly, a Vietnam veteran.

This President, frustrated by diplomacy, is heroic only when he goes *mano-a-mano* with Russian separatists who hijack the eponymous airliner. At the climax of the film, the summative one-liner delivered through gritted Presidential teeth is 'get off my plane' as he literally kicks the terrorist leader to his death. If it is true as Ziauddin Sardar and Meryl Wyn Davies note that American identity is constructed around ideas and symbols which seamlessly transfer from the local to the global, creating a powerful sense of the Universal value of manifest destiny, then there is hardly a clearer example of how Hollywood 'entrenches the American dream and reinforces the dynamics of American mythology' (2004: 148) than this.

The action movie is very effective in dissecting the psychic crises affecting the image of society, nationality and ideology assumed to be 'dominant' at the time of their production. These films reveal such images to be profoundly problematic, not least in that, as Rick Altman argues 'multiple genre practitioners use genres and generic terminology in differing and potentially contradictory ways' (1999: 208). This means that any study of genre must acknowledge the ways that either the genre on the whole or individual genre films are read, perceived or even experienced by those who encounter them.

Much of the anxiety surrounding definition in genre studies stems from the fact that definitions vary depending on the anticipated analytical framework. Barry Keith Grant notes: 'Genre films work by engaging viewers through an implicit contract. They encourage certain expectations on the part of spectators, which are in turn based on viewer familiarity with the conventions' (2007: 21). There is an expectation with the phrase 'action film' that quantifies the prospective experience.

There is a difference between anticipating the pleasures of *Die Hard* (1988) and those of *Raiders of the Lost Ark* (1981). Both are 1980s 'blockbusters' in the mainstream Hollywood mould. Both are redemptive tales of heroism asserting masculinity. Both present active protagonists overcoming obstacles on the journey to personal and social resolution. But they are not the same experience. They do not conjure up the same types and tones of image when the viewer recalls a favourite scene. The image of John McClane repeatedly firing an automatic pistol while swinging away from a high-rise window marked with his own bloody footprints is not congruent with that of Indiana Jones swinging his whip to fend off shaal-enwrapped villains on a backstreet in 1930s Cario. There may be strong Freudian interlinkages between the two, whips and fire hoses and all, but regardless of tempting academic appositions, the films do not 'feel' interchangeable. One is a scene of 'action' the other a moment of 'adventure'.

It is more usual to compress writings on the cinema of action and adventure into a single mould, though Yvonne Tasker does make a distinction between how action 'suggests a sort of filmmaking (in effect, a technique) and a specific set of pleasures' (2004: 7) and adventure 'relates to a kind of story' (ibid.). The aim of this book, the first of two related volumes in the *Short Cuts* series, of which the second will focus on 'adventure', is to facilitate the study of action films by examining the roots of this genre as an embodiment of the idea of action as well as a visualisation and dramatisation of action itself.

It is in this context that Gaylyn Studlar and David Desser express concern regarding the ideological function of action films, with particular reference to *Rambo: First Blood Part II*. The authors liken the cultural reception and absorption of these films to the mythmaking of Nazi Germany. They warn of the 'will to myth' (1988: 9) – the displacement of issues within an actual problem (America's involvement in Vietnam in the first place) to other parts of a discursive framework (the MIA question and concepts of repatriation arising from it), a theme echoed by numerous writers, including Sardar and Wyn Davies (2004). Prince notes of the vigilante film *The Brave One* (2007), set in Manhattan, that the central character's estrangement and alienation from her environment following an attack by muggers who kill her boyfriend consciously refuses reference to 9/11 and yet, 'the thugs' attack is the film's way of coding and transposing this event' (2009: 287). The rise of vengeance narratives in the wake of 9/11 is, Prince observes, a means of articulating 'feelings of violation' (2009: 286) and cauterising the psychic wounds through generic frameworks.

Indeed Neal King argues that the struggle with 'inner demons' so prevalent in the action movie is not just backstory, but part of a moral argument grounding the actions of its characters in societal unease: 'The moral logic of this fictional world merits study because it can offer a version of widespread anger available nowhere else' (1999: 3). Reporting on 'Rambomania' in 1985, Richard Zoglin quoted clinical psychologist Arthur Egendorf, saying 'Rambo is an effort to deal with a complex, painful and deep wound with simple and sentimental responses. Part of the psychological potency of fairy tales such as these is that they dramatize our own inner struggles' (1985). The extent to which the inner and outer struggles mirror one another in terms of the philosophical will, or to which this cinema of crisis dramatises the experience of one for the other, may revolve around notions of genre itself. The concept of genre as 'fairy tale' is explored by Rick Altman, who argues that genres serve both 'ritual' and 'ideological' functions (1999: 26). On one hand genres serve the 'ritual' folk narrative (Egendorf's 'fairy tale') function of giving unity to an audience's view of itself. On the other hand they can be seen to sustain an official 'ideological' political consensus (Rambo posters at US Army recruitment offices). Grant agrees with this assessment, remarking that 'whatever their politics, genre movies are intimately imbricated within larger cultural discourses as well as political ones' (2007: 6).

The question must be asked though: does the appearance of assurance necessarily signify an absence of discourse? Is *Rambo: First Blood Part II* not inherently *about* these things? In raising a moral issue, is it not taking a moral stance, albeit an intellectually unpopular right-wing one? The first two Rambo films clearly articulate rage and frustration. In *First Blood* (1982) the distressed Vietnam veteran lashes out at a society that has betrayed and rejected him by waging a one-man war at home that he loses and for which he is imprisoned. The second film is self-evidently fantastical in sending him back to Vietnam to 'win' the war. But, like the fantasy of the Schwarzenegger *Hamlet*, it represents a decisive action: an attempt to attain agency. Interviewed by Zoglin, Sylvester Stallone remarked: 'So it's a right-wing fantasy. This is the point: frustrated Americans trying to recapture some glory' (in Zoglin 1985). Speaking in 2008, Stallone referred to the genre on the whole as the 'action morality film' (2008: 18). The redemptive discourse is not hidden or insidious.

Rambo: First Blood Part II was not the first morally redemptive Vietnam saga presented in an action mode: it was preceded by *Uncommon Valor* (1983) in which a team of mercenaries are contracted to rescue the son of a wealthy businessman, and *Missing in Action* (1984) in which an American officer defies orders and infiltrates a secret POW camp ten years after his own escape. In being the most spectacularly realised of the three films (even skeptical reviewers found much to admire in Jack Cardiff's cinematography, and Jerry Goldsmth's score came to define the musical soundscape of the era), *Rambo: First Blood Part II* found the biggest audience, but it was, in itself, part of a tide of an emotional response to issues around Vietnam (anger not least) in which the moral logic of the world was painstakingly constructed to enable a sense of righteous indignation and sympathy for Rambo. The fact that Rambo 'wins' the war is less important than the fact that he tries to – *he acts*. In acting he dramatises both the inner struggles of himself and the outer struggles of America on the whole in psychically processing the Vietnam experience.

Might then the opportunity be to examine the action film in terms of what it is doing – how it takes action – rather than presuppose that such analysis must of necessity begin with an overarching framework defined beyond (and in opposition with) the text itself? Tasker cautions against dismissal of the obviousness of the action film on the grounds that 'Analysis of the films has little significance if one accepts the premise that there is nothing to be said about them' (1993: 8). These are genre films, and yet, she notes, the articulate, verbal, liberal critical response to the film generated a climate of intellectual interrogation. She asks, bearing this in mind, 'what is at stake in the processes whereby the popular cinema becomes the object of concerned analysis?' (1993: 108).

There is an inherent expressivity in action that comes from its association with movement. Aaron Anderson (1998) deploys the term 'kinesthesia' to describe the interconnection between physical, textual and sensual action upon which the pleasure of action films is based. Kinesthesia can be defined as pertaining to the sensations generated by the relationship between muscles, tendons and joints and the senses that detect these physical relationships. It is a term most frequently used in analysis of an understanding of dance. Anderson deploys it in his essay on the cinema of Steven Seagal. He critiques standard approaches to Hollywood action movies, including that of Tasker, in terms of the theorising of body practices where, as he argues, the focus on iconic, imagistic muscularity is at the expense of any sense of the use and sensation of those muscles in motion and in sequence.

Anderson, a former soldier, begins by describing a scene from his own basic training where trainees were shown Bruce Lee's *Enter the Dragon* (1973) the night before a physical training examination. The purpose of the screening was not merely to motivate the trainees psychologically, but to stimulate them physically − to trigger their trained bodies to emulate what they had seen and to generate sensation from viewing the representation of movement and trigger a desire to move. As he puts it, 'Our mental association with the invincible character we saw on screen expressed itself through our own physical actions as we consciously attempted to recreate elements of Lee's movements within our own bodies. This physical recreation of movement, in turn, constituted a type of muscular memory' (1998: 1). He argues that the kinesthetic sensation triggered by representations of action is as important as other textual aspects, and that the role of 'muscular memory' is at the heart of how audiences respond viscerally to action films.

Hong Kong martial arts films, of which *Enter the Dragon* was a transnational offshoot, were almost always written of in the West by likening their staging of fights to dance choreography. Writing as early as 1974, Tony

Kinesthetic emulation: Bruce Lee in *Enter the Dragon* (1973)

Rayns remarked that 'the Chinese have established a new visual rhetoric for the presentation of hand-to-hand combat on film' (1974: 139). Fights, he says, 'are staged like a cross between acrobatics and ballet, with great sweeps of action carried through a crowd of performers. The likeness to dance is heightened by most directors' use of slow-motion inserts to pick out the precisely choreographed movements in detail' (ibid.). David Bordwell takes this even further. He remarks on the importance of clarity of movement in Hong Kong cinema emerging out of its theatrical tradition (the Peking Opera), but makes the point that movement is then further enhanced by *cinematographic* movement – in cutting, composition, colour and sound. He describes what he calls 'a strategy of expressive ampli-fication' (2000: 232) through which gesture and facial expression are deployed not to convey nuance, but to make any given image even more communicative, which, in his words 'magnifies the emotional dynamics of the performance' (ibid.).

Anderson analyses the relationship between cinematic martial arts and kinesthesia in similar terms to Bordwell. He outlines the narrational function of movement and its expressive qualities on an emotional level, but also presents a more evolved sense of the nature of the body, trained and untrained, and how this relates to audience response as well as the film text itself 'in action'. Seagal's actual grounding in Aikido, the Japanese martial art that focuses on the redirection of energy through fluid responses marking his mode of action as a reaction. This is something of an ideal paradigmatic analogy for the conception of action proposed in this book. As a villain moves to strike him, Seagal will sidestep, grasp the offending limb and assume control of it using the intertia of the original action to turn the act of violence back on itself.

Even if untrained, humans share a sense of how bodies move. Watching the flow of movement, particularly in a martial arts film, enables an under-standing of what a represented movement might feel like (think of the clas-sic sympathetic male response to injuries to the groin depicted in films or television). Action films rely heavily upon this kind of response, using what Bordwell would describe as strategies of expressive amplification to empha-sise edits on action and enhance the sense of movement and violence, to produce the kind of empathetic response Anderson is talking about.

Anderson is acutely aware of the philosophical and social dimension of the staging of physical action. He observes: 'Philosophers through the ages have wrestled with the juxtaposition of psyche and body without clear success. In contrast, all theories of kinesthetics imply that the Cartesian split represents a false dichotomy. Kinesthetic theories assert that certain mental or psychical elements have physical manifestations and that certain physical movements likewise have mental or psychical referents' (1998: 11). He points out, for example, that in narrative terms, almost any given combat is essentially redundant in a Seagal film (and this is true of all martial arts films), but particularly in the example he gives: *Out for Justice* (1991). Here lithe, young, angry cop Seagal fights 'fat and slow' (ibid.) drug lord William Forsythe at the film's climax. The outcome is never in doubt, but the battle involves a number of specific physical actions; kicks and punches, blows and blocks, challenges and responses that Seagal's character must undergo because, as Anderson says, 'the kinesthetic effect itself is the primary focus of the scene' (ibid.).

In this he is making the vital point that action films are literally and figuratively *in a state of action* which requires audience engagement with that action not as a static 'spectacle' playing out in tableau, but as a dynamic sequence of expressive amplification which they 'feel' though an empathetic kinesthetic effect. Furthermore, this sense of engagement relies upon the audience not so much suspending their involvement with narrative as knowing that the action they are seeing constitutes a significant part of their sensory experience of the film as text and as genre. Victory proves the hero's worth in a manner, as Anderson observes, 'reminiscent of a medieval trial by combat in which God alone is judge' (ibid.), but the film requires the battle *to be seen* to satisfactorily resolve the audience's desire to see the character *in the act of being tested*.

The potential to read action movies not merely in terms of their textual outcomes, but of the struggles that they depict as struggles in action (that which constitutes action and that which is acted upon) is what locates these films within the culture and politics of their production, where they are 'in action'. These are active texts, literally *active*. We can see here that it is only by engaging with that action as action in itself, considering both volition and teleology as markers of agency in that action, that we can begin to find these films to be a particular configuration of text and aesthetic definitive of at least a mode of address, if not a genre. In acknowledging this, we may critically engage with these films armed with new analytical weapons.

A Selective History of the Action Movie

So many films contain, feature or are even built around action that the phrase 'action movie' is tautological. It could serve a synonym for cinema itself, and does (or used to): 'motion picture'. The very word 'cinema' is derived from a word connoting a type of action – movement (from the Greek 'kine'), making all cinema 'action'. Cinema began with action, and some of its earliest hits involved an empathic kinesthetic response. Early boxing films inspired audience members to re-stage the events on screen, and films of dance, acrobatics and even martial arts demonstrated the primacy of action *as* action in the experience of cinema itself. None of this describes the genre of 'action movies' though, and so we will of necessity dispense with overly mapping its roots throughout the entirety of cinematic history.

That said the action film may be seen to emerge historically through a prism of other genres – primarily the western, the crime film and the war movie – which fuse through the 1970s into an identifiable register of form and content by the early 1980s. The history of the action film may therefore be divided into evolutionary stages with a rough chronology falling into formative, classical, postclassical and neoclassical phases. The first phase dates generally from the late 1960s to the early 1980s, during which the anti-hero emerges as a figure of agency; a character who willfully embraces the necessity to take action and transcend not only social convention, but law and legitimacy. Society becomes a moral battleground on which social tensions played out against a sensibility of virtually psychotic individuality. Though this is initially framed as protecting society (in *Bullitt* (1968) a tough cop attempts to uphold the law against systematic corruption), it is evident that the action hero is trying to preserve aspects of self and social identity irredeemable in the light of contemporary values (in *First Blood* a rejected Vietnam veteran lashes out). This is also a pathological reaction; a knee-jerk response to perceived threats to the dominant order, and this becomes the subject of the rogue cop and vigilante films through *Dirty Harry* (1971) and *Death Wish* (1974), which visit personal trauma as the site of teleology. Here the restoration of order is only possible by the exertion of (necessary) force by anti-social or at least anti-heroic characters prepared to act when society will not.

This has a direct link with the rise of mercenary narratives, which also correspond historically with the employment of private military by globalising corporations, in which action becomes internationalised and politicised. Films like *The Wild Geese* (1978) and *The Dogs of War* (1980) present corporate neoimperialism as the hot front of the Cold War – covert action outside the machinations of legitimate political confrontation in which moral values are negotiated through economic interests.

Vigilantism is elevated to the level of a cultural alternative in the 'Southern Exploitation' sub-genre, which also emerges at this time, positing a rebel society with roots in American historical schisms. If the vigilante and rogue cop films could be spoken of as 'urban westerns', there emerged a thread of neo-western (by way of the South), through *Billy Jack* (1971), *White Lightning* (1973) and *Walking Tall* (1973), culminating in the 'good ol' boy' comedies of the later 1970s like *Smokey and the Bandit* (1977), most of which were also, significantly, car chase movies.

The period also sees the evolution of a new cinematic syntax of action through its emphasis on the fusion of man and machine. Car chase scenes presented as moments of spectacle in films including *Bullitt* and *The French Connection* (1971) gradually assume a virtually nihilistic sense of post-human erasure through *Two-Lane Blacktop* (1971) and *The Driver* (1978), culminating in the ultimate in apocalyptic modernity and social erasure in favour of an image of individualism in *Mad Max 2* (1981). The logistical requirements of realising these narratives cinematically, literalising the image of man and machine moving and acting as one, necessitates the development of staging, shooting and editing techniques to make films built entirely around movement and action, an expressive amplification that again makes sense in Bordwell and Anderson's terms on the level of kinesthesia.

The second phase of historical development in the genre is the consolidation of its 'classical' period in the 1980s. As the body becomes the machine, the intensified continuity system used to film cars in the 1970s now captures bodies in motion – weaponised men (armed (*Sudden Impact*, 1983); trained (*American Ninja*, 1985); even technologically enhanced (*Robocop*, 1987)) and framed by architectural musculature. All of the thematic tensions of the preceding era remained prevalent, as did the characterisation of heroes as avengers (*Lethal Weapon*, 1987), rogue cops (*Die Hard*, 1988) and mercenary warriors (*Commando*, 1985), but now the structures become identifiably generic. The genre itself becomes a machine as the industry commodifies and efficiently reproduces the delivery system for action-filled tales of action. Producers and production companies like the Cannon Group and Joel Silver quickly recognised and seized upon the 'formula' and begin to generate product at high and low budgetary levels following a simple set of structuring conventions.

The classical action movie is built around a three-act structure centred on survival, resistance and revenge. It is a narrative of social and personal redemption in which the act of will is embodied in the physical body of the hero – tested, traumatised and triumphant. Its motifs of body condition-ing, injury and repair clearly delineate a deeper cultural attitude towards masculinity and agency, presenting a positive (if mildly psychotic) outlook, arguably expressed *in extremis*. Cause and effect narratives are structured around scenes of violent action in which the nemesis (villain) enacts or inflicts damage which threatens the survival (and status) of the hero, requiring an increasingly challenging series of responses moving from ini-tially surviving the threat, then to actively resisting it, to finally overcoming it and vanquishing (and punishing) the nemesis.

It is not the most distinctive of generic structures (with clear correla-tions with classic narrative), nor is it the most subtle, but subtlety is not the point. These films express a conscious articulation of the desire to act – to respond to the nemesis and eliminate the threat. *Predator* (1987) is one of the clearest articulations of this theme in one of its most cleanly primal realisations: a tale of an elite mercenary battling an alien hunter in a dense jungle in which man achieves victory only when stripped of technology and given the pure motivation of survival. As the alien kills more and more of the team, layers of meaning are taken away (the 'political' plot, the 'rescue' narrative – the trappings of justification and context) – leaving Dutch (Arnold Schwarzenegger) literally stripped to his skin, caked in mud, and screaming a wordless roar of challenge across the jungle: come and get me, I'm ready.

The story structure has roots not only in classical storytelling, but specifi-cally the martial arts film and the western. It should come as little surprise that fusions with the Eastern traditions began as early as *Enter the Dragon* and grew particularly through the films of Chuck Norris, most notably *Lone Wolf McQuade* (1983), where the fusion of hard-body Western (and 'west-ern' genre) tropes and martial arts vengeance narrative was made seamless via Norris's persona. The climactic showdown between Norris and David Carradine, who had achieved fame playing the serene (Asian) hero of the television series *Kung Fu* (1972–75), was anything but incidental.

When the Bogeyman goes to bed, he checks his closet for Chuck Norris: Norris vs. Carradine in *Lone Wolf McQuade* (1983)

The third significant shift in the action film was defined by a gradual predominance of Eastern aesthetic motifs and staging conventions through the increasing deployment of computer-generated effects, particularly the fantastical 'wire-work' style of Hong Kong films of the previous era. As Hong Kong itself faced its political transition, the migration of Asian directors to Hollywood facilitated the exceeding of the conditions of body that had predominated in the 1980s. As Clinton-era postmodernity evinced a 'softer' or at least more mediated political stance in American genre cinema, the hard body gave way to an evolved body capable of impossible physical feats with the aid of digital enhancement.

As the deployment of computer-generated imagery in *Terminator 2: Judgement Day* (1991) demonstrated, form was relative, and the imaginings of the digital shifted the action from from the realm of wish-fulfillment to actual fantasy. The disconnection from the primacy of kinesthetic effects came to manifest itself not merely in ever-more elaborate and increasingly spectacular films that tended towards fantasy, science fiction and adventure, but also a collapse into self-referentiality, parody, and self-erasure, most notably in *Last Action Hero*, in which the implosion of tropes was not only evident, but a conscious theme. This era saw the decline of the hysterically monolithic masculinities of the classical period (corresponding with the end of the Cold War) and the growth of a post-classical meta-masculinity framed by a seemingly limitless imaginary (or a negotiation with the impossible).

This was, of course, also a reactive configuration of the capacity of humanity itself, and corresponds with millennial angst and apocalypticism culminating in narratives of disaster and destruction like *Independence Day* (1996), *Titanic* (1997) and *Armageddon* (1998). Spectacles of mass destruction required literally super-heroic characters to respond and regain control, evinced by the success of comic book adaptations and an increased emphasis on fantasy settings suggesting a desire for the apotheosis of the action hero. This was arguably literalised with Neo's assumption of a Messianic role in *The Matrix* (1999), which culminates in the character's 'resurrection' as he learns to control the forces of reality itself.

The events of 11 September 2001 suggested an end to fantasy, or at least to the fantasies of volition that defined the action hero and the action movie, and yet it did not take long for the genre to in fact experience something of a renaissance, or, in the parlance of the moment, 'reboot'. Vengeance narratives like *The Brave One* and *Taken* (2008) revisited many of the traumatic tropes of their 1970s forebears, while Steven Spielberg's *Munich* (2005) showed these same tropes and structures to serve focused, dramatic and politicised grounding in assessing the legacies of violence. Meanwhile Quentin Tarantino's *Kill Bill: Vol. 1* (2003) and *Kill Bill: Vol. 2* (2004) revisited these same tropes through an active, arguably deconstructive postmodernism that transcended irony to restore cinephilic reactualisation of the genre's conventions.

Finally, the genre seemed to come full circle in narratives of restoration, repatriation and redemption that now encompassed not only historical context but cinematic history too as *Die Hard 4.0* (2007) and the confusingly-titled *Rambo* (2008) resurrected iconic action heroes from the 1980s and placed them in hostile negotiation with the contemporary world. These heroes remained reactive, decisive and victorious, but also acknowledged their age. This is indicative of a genre on an evolutionary cycle: not in a state of termination, but renewal. Sylvester Stallone's *The Expendables* (2010), then, seems an apt summation of the formal and historical trajectory of the genre, in which Stallone as director facilitates the fusion of contemporary and classic cast members in an avowedly 'old school' mercenary narrative. Equally though, Clint Eastwood's *Gran Tornio* (2008) offered an alternative vision of ideological renewal, presenting an appeal to the roots of the action hero's driving necessity to see justice done by understanding the society in whose name justice is sought. This elegiac farewell to old paradigms came nonetheless with a confident assertion of the desire to watch men of action take action, and even endure injury in the process, to the extent of opening out the 'reaction' to heroes as yet unrealised and perhaps inconceivable to an intransigent ideology.

This book explores this loose historical trajectory within a given set of overall themes – the ideology of conflict, social opposition and individuality, the role of the (gendered, racialised) body, the collapse of ideological framing, and finally the paradox of 'the return'. The purpose of the book is to open debate and introduce avenues of exploration and discourse that will enrich responses to this most disreputable of genres, and in doing so broaden perspective in ways which perhaps will not make Jack Slater into Hamlet, but indicate the means by which the juxtaposition of the two may not seem so entirely incongruous as a conceptualisation of what it means to take action.

1 THE WAR AT HOME

The Urban Western: Rogue Cops and Vigilante Avengers

In *Death Wish* Paul Kersey (Charles Bronson), an architect whose wife has been murdered and daughter raped, becomes a vigilante. Though an educated pacifist, Kersey has snapped in the face of his sense of power-lessness. During a business trip to Arizona he discovers an aptitude for firearms after he attends a Wild West show with a client, who makes him a gift of a .32 revolver. Kersey's sense of morality, honour and even heroism is framed by a delusion, referencing received images of strength, will and 'frontier justice', driven by trauma and psychosis. At the film's climax, a wounded Kersey pursues a mugger to an abandoned train yard. Bleeding, tiring, delirium overtaking him, Kersey draws a bead on his target and says 'Fill your hand.' The mugger has no idea what he means.

 The command to 'fill your hand' is an invitation to battle: a reference to *True Grit* (1969) in which an aging John Wayne plays Rooster Cogburn, a US Marshall who faces down four gunmen in a bravura climax where the line is spoken in response to an agist insult leveled against him. In Cogburn's case this battle requires significant strength – four young men against a single 'one-eyed fat man'. In Kersey's case, it is an ironic line as the mugger is unarmed and Kersey has spent the entire film summarily executing similar street punks in an act of universal vengeance (these are not even the perpetrators of the crimes against his family). It is also, in the event, an impotent line, as he falls unconscious and his quarry escapes.

Reviewing *Death Wish* in *Newsweek* in 1974 Maureen Orth described the film as 'an urban western' (see Talbot 2006: 21). Though Will Wright wrote confidently of the mythic function of the American western, concluding it 'contains a conceptual analysis of society that provides a model of social action' (1975: 185) there were few new films to write about. The western was dying as a genre, arguably facing total erasure after *The Wild Bunch* (1969) eviscerated its mythology with a cautionary tale of anachronism and extinction.

By the late 1960s American cinema had begun to reflect the uneasy sensibility of the post-Kennedy years. It was a cinema of doubt, framed by a society seemingly on the brink of revolution. These were the years of the 'war at home' where political unrest resulting from counter-cultural resistance to the Vietnam War led to a series of intense confrontations with governmental authority, leading often to social unrest and even violence. Many of the films of this period demonstrate a sense of social tension between heroic ideals and social values, sometimes to the detriment of established genres whose tenets had been evolved in a completely different social paradigm, particularly war films and westerns.

Wright identifies four plot structures, all revolving around the status of the hero relative to individual and social values: in the 'classical' plot the hero aids society by joining with it; in 'the vengeance variation' he begins within society but steps outside because it is too weak to permit his pursuit of vengeance; in 'the transitional theme' he leaves society because it is too strong and too much at odds with his (heroic) worldview; in 'the professional plot' he protects society simply because he has been paid (1975: 29–123). All four of these structures recur in non-western films throughout the 1970s. The fact is that the change in historical framework and iconography is not incidental, and produces subtle variations on the relatively clear-cut moral parameters of the western genre, not least of all because the postmodern geographies (physical and psychic) involved cannot but shift the mythic paradigm from classical models.

Wright's 'model of social action' was still applicable to these and subsequent films as the historical and iconographical frames of reference shifted towards modernity and urban space. The underlying themes of social action and social order in the light of an evolving civilisation are consistent, but there is a change in perspective with the shift to the urban that resonated with contemporary audiences. An 'urban western' is 'urban' first, representing the physical landscape of present experience as a marker of 'civilisation' instead of using nineteenth-century frontier imagery as a cipher for the same thing. As Ed Buscombe puts it 'the city became the frontier, and the savages – the muggers and rapists – were already inside the gates' (1993: 53). The capacity to navigate this dangerous space is one of the markers of the action hero, as is the (post-)modernistic fascination with urban imagery (helicopter shots of cityscapes, alienating juxtapositions between actors and surrounding buildings). Even the visual palette of *Death Wish* evokes not so much a documentary image of New York in the early 1970s commensurate with crime dramas, but more an expressionistic labyrinth of twisting alleyways filled with lurking dangers reflecting Kersey's paranoid fantasy. It is significant that Kersey is an architect (an accountant in the original novel), reinforcing the western's concern with the literal building of civilisation. Kersey designs spaces to be lived in, only to find that those who dwell in architectural spaces may not conform to social design.

Coogan's Bluff may be the exemplary urban western in its deployment of a dual architecture of contemporary crime drama and classic western. Clint Eastwood plays Arizona Deputy Sheriff Walt Coogan, sent to New York to extradite a criminal, but finding himself baffled by the social and physical environment. Eastwood's unapologetically classical westerner is pitted against the sins of the 'civilised' East, thoroughly overrun by criminality, immorality and hedonism, but also against the bureaucratic authorities that insist on deference to the procedures of modern law enforcement. Eventually Coogan is able to navigate through the urban jungle and escape from it – a literal flight back to his 'civilisation' which is clearly (and nostalgically) encoded as a social, sexual and cinematic past.

The opening scene enacts the drama of confrontation between classic and contemporary iconography as Coogan brings in a Navajo fugitive. There is conscious deference to the classic western in the desert landscape and the Native American lurking in the brush. The paraphernalia of modernity is then brought to bear, firstly in the semi-automatic rifle with a telescopic sight carried by the Navajo, then in the form of Coogan's jeep, which is seen tearing across the landscape and used to stir up dust and prevent the Navajo from getting a clear shot.

This scenario is replayed in reverse throughout the film as Coogan becomes disenfranchised from the environment. In New York Coogan is

Eastern decadence under the western gaze: Clint Eastwood confronts the counter-culture in *Coogan's Bluff* (1968)

overwhelmed by the new urban architecture and its culture and is literally attacked by the contemporary counter-culture. When he enters a club called 'Pidgeon-Toed Orange Peel' he is confronted by psychedelic lights and music illustrating scenes of sexual deviance including nudity and homosexuality. There he meets Linny Raven (Tisha Sterling), his quarry's hippy girlfriend who has sex with him, but then arranges for Coogan to be beaten up. He later attacks her, throwing her around her beaded, mural-decorated apartment before throttling her in front of a huge painting of the word 'love', and driving his fist through the wall beside her head.

In Linny we have, as Alan Lovell remarks, one of director Don Siegel's 'women who convert their unbalanced sexual desires and envies into violence' (1975: 37) and a doubling of the film's skepticism with modernity and sexual identity. Her refusal of the dominant orthodoxy of desire, where she should fall in love with the manly hero and share his values, is represented as criminal impulse. This becomes a register of the trauma of the sexual revolution, here clearly being reacted against by a hero who takes direct action – crushing the liberal sensibility. In doing so, he is seen also to re-ignite the traditional domesticated desire of the heroine, initially liberal and progressive probation officer Julie Roth (Susan Clark), who waves a teary goodbye to the gunfighter at the film's conclusion as he rides off into the proverbial sunset, albeit in a helicopter.

Dirty Harry, also directed by Don Siegel, would cement Eastwood as the defining urban cowboy, and would provide the template for the 'rogue cop' movie that would become one of the foundations of the action genre. In it San Francisco Detective Inspector Harry Callahan (Eastwood) pursues a killer called Scorpio (Andy Robinson) in defiance of the rules of due process. Callahan's confrontations with his superiors are as much the focus of the film as the battle with Scorpio. They represent a consistent and repeated punctuation of the narrative – a restraint of action that merely makes the audience anticipate the film's cathartic explosions of violence when Harry is unleashed (this was precisely what the film's tagline promised – 'You don't assign Harry to murder cases, you turn him loose.') When Harry disobeys orders, confronts and kills Scorpio and then throws away his badge at the end of the film, he has taken action, but abandoned the civilisation he has upheld. Unlike Coogan though, he has nowhere to return to where he is socially legitimate.

That Harry represented the new breed of urban enforcer stepping almost unreconstructed out of western myth is barely debatable, certainly when you compare the film with *The French Connection*, released the same year. *The French Connection* loosely follows the true story of New York's biggest ever drugs bust as Detective Jimmy 'Popeye' Doyle (Gene Hackman) pursues a complex chain of evidence through thugs and street dealers to mastermind Alan Charnier (Fernando Rey). *The French Connection* took the crime film towards the more realistic 'New Hollywood' aesthetic in its depiction of New York; *Dirty Harry* remained in the figurative and literal West. *The French Connection* is about solving a complex crime through dogged determination and investigative police work; *Dirty Harry* is about solving all crime, as represented by a single murderer, through decisive action and the application of extreme force, including harassment and torture. Two very different visions of civilisation are being upheld here. Though aspects of the same configurations of tensions between heroism, civilisation and landscape as outlined in *Dirty Harry* are present in *The French Connection*, its 'rogue cop' is also, in spite of himself, more integrated with the system, and this is precisely what gives the film its *frisson* in the final scene where Doyle's sanity and perhaps criminal culpability in seeking vengeance is left unresolved.

Dirty Harry triggered critical and cultural debate around the politics of this emergent cinematic sensibility. Writing in *The New Yorker*, perennially acerbic critic Pauline Kael described it as both fascist and immoral, making the film a hot button for public discourse. In fact Kael remarked that the action film on the whole had always had 'fascist potential' (1985: 148), but that *Dirty Harry* had brought it to the surface. This remark encapsulates the situation of this emergent cinematic sensibility at this juncture in history. The action film marks an explicit emergence of a reactionary panic to a perceived threat to social order; one, ironically, hereby symbolically contained by violence wielded in the name of that same order but in opposition to its 'civilised' tenets. This would endure throughout the following years, across numerous direct *Dirty Harry* sequels, and various re-iterations of the formula with varying degrees of subtlety. Certainly there was little but blunt rhetoric in the advertising for the Sylvester Stallone vehicle *Cobra* (1986): 'Crime is a disease. Meet the Cure.'

Films in which ordinary citizens take the law into their own hands are quite different than the 'rogue cop' variety, although examples of the vigilante film still fall within the same framework – arguably shifting focus from the cowboys to the outlaws. In fact, the difference cuts to the heart of discourses of law and order in American history. David Johnson reports that in the 1860s San Francisco, where *Dirty Harry* is set, was one of the most active centres of vigilante activity in the United States. At that time 'vigilance committees' and frontier justice operated quasi-legitimately in a legal and judicial system attempting to regulate an evolving society (1981: 561). Johnson points out that the struggle to establish a system of judicial law throughout the nineteenth century hinged on a shift between what was perceived as natural justice and the actual rule of law from an integrated legislative authority. What is therefore at stake in the vigilante film is the rule of man versus the rule of law and the sense of self-determination and the capacity for action that comes with it.

This is in play in *Death Wish* where, not unlike its 'rogue cop' forebears, a bureaucratic police force and a seemingly immobile but frustrated populace needs an agent of action to respond to the threat of urban crime. The loose cannon here is a free agent, but one that operates with the tacit approval of professional authority. Throughout the film street crime decreases as Kersey's rampage progresses, and the police debate whether or not to allow the vigilante to continue his activities. This culminates in a scene where, as Kersey lies in hospital recovering from his wounds, wizened police detective Frank Ochoa (Vincent Gardenia) advises him to get out of town. In response Kersey quips 'by sundown?' In using this particular line and in emphasising Kersey's reaction to the reconstructed western street fight he sees in Tuscon the legacy of the western as the locus of 'frontier justice' as text, as trope and as social construction is made eminently clear.

While urban westerns may have adopted the tropes and devices of the classic western, rural (or at least non-urban) American imagery did not completely disappear. In fact, a 'new western' strain of a type developed alongside these sharing many of the same concerns. Vigilante films like *Billy Jack* and *Walking Tall* can also be located at least partly within a so-called 'Southern exploitation' mould. Scott Von Doviak argues that this sub-genre can be read as a modern rural American folkloric cinema. He suggests the success of these films may be seen relative to the continued success of blaxploitation films and urban westerns 'providing heroes and myths for those trapped in the inner cities' (2005: 9). The Southern exploitation film, by contrast, serviced drive-ins and scattered rural venues where they spoke to their audience by 'tapping into a recent past all but obliterated by Wal-Marts and strip malls' (ibid.) with a prevalence of rural or backwoods imagery and stories involving renegades, outsiders and miscreants who prove heroic in their defiance of 'civilised' (Northern) values. In this way the acts of vigilante justice and social cleansing carried out by the protagonists of these films form an even stronger link between the anti-hero and social agency. These characters earn their social mandate by dint of the unwelcome domination of a modernising urban culture, which these films unfailingly portray as corrupt and destructive.

This is the focus of the *Billy Jack* series, mostly written, produced, directed by and starring Tom Laughlin. The films are quixotic tales of a peaceful liberal cowboy (and, it is eventually revealed, a Vietnam veteran) pushed beyond his limits by the intrusions of state authorities. Only *The Born Losers* (1967) deploys traditional outlaw villains – a biker gang (the contemporary cinema's analogue for the raiding Indian bands of the classic western). In *Billy Jack* the opposition is the wealthy landowner who pressures a local 'freedom school' with the collusion of local authorities. In *The Trial of Billy Jack* (1974), Laughlin broadens the palette to include fictive dramatisations of the real-life Kent State Shootings as governmental authorities move to repress liberal education, and *Billy Jack Goes to Washington* (1977) more or less speaks for itself. Throughout all of these films, it is social institutions that represent systematised violence and repression, in an illustration of what Slavoj Žižek describes as 'the often catastrophic consequences of the smooth functioning of our economic and political systems' (2008: 1). In these terms Billy Jack's assumption of agency represents a reaction against centrist social consensus. Significantly in genre terms, this reaction is realised not only as politicised action, but actual combat.

The most exciting sequences in each of the *Billy Jack* films are the martial arts battles. These demonstrate both the tutelage of Hapkido master Bong Soo Han, who trained Laughlin, and a comparatively early adoption of some of the cinematic architecture of Hong Kong martial arts films. This is particularly pointed in *Billy Jack* when Billy and his students are taunted in an ice cream parlour, causing Billy to call out the local thugs to the nearby park. A series of establishing shots from above establish the geographical boundaries of the combat, showing Billy at the centre of a circle of antagonists, before the film intercuts to images of individual blows and kicks as he fights. The editing is not as fluid, nor are Laughlin's movements as quick or graceful, as his Asian counterparts, but the very 'heaviness' of the blows is more visually resonant with John Wayne than Bruce Lee, and this may be the point, as it was later in the films of Chuck Norris.

Walking Tall also spawned a series of films, and, many years on, a remake (2004) and second series of sequels released direct to video. *Walking Tall* is a rogue cop movie in that it dramatises the real-life story of Sheriff Buford Pusser, who began a one-man crusade against moonshine and gambling in rural Tennessee in the mid-1960s. The film takes its narrative dynamics primarily from *High Noon* (1952) by having Pusser (Joe Don Baker) struggle as much to gain social acceptance for his crusade (and his campaign for Sheriff) as against the forces of civil disorder (shown to be in collusion with corrupt local authority). The film is marked by a number of scenes of violent action that, like in *Billy Jack*, are its kinesthetic engine. Buford responds to the frustrations of corruption by direct action, first of all violence (armed with a trademark wooden club he literally sets out to 'smash' corruption), then with political action when he runs for and becomes Sheriff, then again with violence, as he crushes illegality, now legitimised by legal authority.

Walking Tall revels in a sense of pride in the purity of authentic local culture. Pusser returns to Tennessee after a successful career as a wrestler, seeking a peaceful life. His location within a happy family (shattered by violence when his wife is killed), eventually in a job with civic responsibility, and particularly his impassioned speech during a key courtroom scene in which he appeals to the jury to 'remember there's still a little law and order left' positions Pusser on the side of moral rightness and civic renewal and those against him on the side of venality associated with degraded modernity. This is not to suggest that rural values are atavistic, but certainly they are grounded in tradition: particularly family, but also community. However in *Deliverance* (1972) and *Southern Comfort* (1981), atavism is precisely how such communities are defined, and the reverse scenario played out as a critique of the ethic of action sees modern would-be warriors (businessmen on an adventure trip, Army reservists) discovering that their fantasies of mastery fall afoul of embedded cultures, represented as deranged 'others'. It is a clear Vietnam metaphor, but it is interesting that in both cases it is the rural South of the United States, locus of these other more redemptive tales of independent spirit, that proves the quagmire from which the failed heroes cannot emerge.

Both the concept of community and the character of the liberal avenger are thrown into relief by Sam Peckinpah's *Straw Dogs* (1971). In it American mathematician David Sumner (Dustin Hoffman), a proverbially mild-mannered, pacifist intellectual, moves away from strife-torn America to a country house in rural England with his beautiful British wife Amy (Susan George). Her overt sexuality eventually enflames the desires of local ruffians, who continually harass the couple before finally raping Amy and laying siege to the farmhouse, causing the pacifist to become an avenger.

It is, as *Sight & Sound* dismissed it, a 'thesis film' (Shaffer 1972: 133), and plays out Peckinpah's characteristic concern with the struggle to retain individual identity in the face of social change. It is also, Charles Barr argues, a film which encourages the viewer 'to face, think through, feel through the implications of human aggression' (1972: 29), not least of all in the extremity of the provocation to David's pacifism. As Barr observes, David's comparatively sheltered and privileged sense of the world makes his pacifism a form of denial, and in confronting the violence within himself as well as with those around him, David's intellectual principles are truly tested. As Peckinpah himself said: 'An intellectual who embodies his intellect in action, that's a real human being' (see Andrews 1973: 74).

The film's connection with the traditional western is reinforced by its rural setting though its contemporaneity is signalled by a geographical transition of that rurality to modern England. Audiences are able to reconcile the rural imagery with the experience of modernity and also connect it with the contemporary American experience of expatriate alienation, at least partly because of the flight of so many young men avoiding the military draft. In this though the rural dystopia may have the character of metaphor, it is presented as a living location. This provides the film with a premise for discourse on the concept of a 'home', as in a place within which one can locate oneself and establish one's own identity (again, a western trope), to which 'war' is brought.

As in *Walking Tall*, the domestic idyll is shattered by what happens, and at the film's end an important conversation occurs between David and local yokel Henry (David Warner). When Henry despairingly remarks that he doesn't know his way home, David replies 'I don't either.' This restates the sense of isolation created by the finale of *Dirty Harry*: David, like Harry, has no sense of home. He finds himself isolated from civilisation as a man who has taken action to defend his physical integrity, though perhaps at the cost of an intellectual principle.

Intellectual (and moral) principles are also at stake in *Death Wish*, which, as previously mentioned, offers a central character nominally enwrapped in the rhetoric of the liberal left. Kersey explains to his gun-toting client (Stuart Margolin) at the Tucson firing range that he was a conscientious objector during the Korean War and, further, that his father, a gun enthusiast, was killed in a hunting accident when Kersey was a child. The film thereby presents an historical legacy of violence nominally rejected

Signs of death: Charles Bronson takes aim in *Death Wish* (1974)

by its protagonist but finally embraced. In contrast to *Straw Dogs* where David feels lost and abandoned as a result of embracing his inner demons, Kersey is shown to be energised by it. In the film's final scene he arrives in Chicago having been quietly let go by the New York police. When a group of young thugs at the train station give him the finger, his response is a gesture of his own – he makes a pretend gun from his fingers and mimes shooting them down, a smile on his face. This is a considerably queasier political message than the fantasy of the maverick cop, anti-heroic well beyond *Dirty Harry*, moving even beyond Wright's 'professional plot' as the agent of social order isn't even hired or employed, but merely acts when, where and how others will not.

Warriors of the Wasteland

For a truer application of Wright's professional plot, it is more appropriate to turn to the mercenary film. Though it too has its roots in westerns, where heroic 'hired guns' were the focus of major films including *The Magnificent Seven* (1960) and *The Professionals* (1966), from the late 1960s more contemporary military-themed mercenary films such as *The Dark of the Sun* (1968) and *Universal Soldier* (1971) emerged, as did the real-life deployment of mercenary armies in global conflicts.

Christopher Kinsey notes that it was the events of 1968 and the subsequent surge in revolutionary terrorist activity around the globe that gave impetus for the growth of private military firms. Capitalist corporations fearing for their safety in revolutionary 'hot zones' began to employ private security. It was only a matter of time before governments also began to deploy mercenaries to protect their interests abroad. There is a fine line between what Kinsey describes as the companies' sense of their role as 'nothing more than holding the line for the international community while it prepares to intervene' (2007: 104) and a reaction of panic and moral convenience on the part of the international community by allowing the veneer of diplomatic process to continue while military personnel are, in fact, present in the region. The simplest example of why this is problematic is to think of the 'police action' in Vietnam, which did not 'hold' and eventually escalated into full-scale war.

Though Neill Hicks is quick to ascribe a 'birthright' (2002: 62) to the action film out of the western and crime paradigms, he neglects the patrimony of the war film. Guy Westwell (2006) argues that the war film occupies a central role in analysing hegemonic discourse at least partly because of its instrumental role as a vehicle of propaganda. By the late 1960s, the ongoing military conflict in Vietnam did not sit well with the continued celebration of the triumphs of World War II. When John Wayne made a heartfelt but misguided attempt to directly represent the conflict in South East Asia in *The Green Berets* (1968) with the full support of the US Army, the real-world historical background of My-Lai and the increasing tensions of the war at home merely underlined the hollowness of the genre's narrative and ideological formulae.

The traditional war film can be distinguished from its successor very simply. The notion of 'legitimacy' inherent in representations of military conflict, at least until the period in question, was given force by the historical specificity and the continued focus on wars and warfare still deemed morally righteous and socially redemptive, primarily World War II. As Lawrence Suid points out, 'for the most part, war movies allow audiences to leave the theatre with a sense of pride in their military men and their country' (2002: 673). That said, Dana Polan argues that part of what makes a war movie work is the conscious, deliberate and articulated meaning assumed by the fact that the given 'mission' of the soldier protagonists necessarily corresponds with the national mission of the war effort, and, as he says 'its purpose was evident, inevitable' (2005: 55). But with Vietnam lost and the notion of national service dead in the United States, the assumption of legitimacy of any war was in question, as were the logistics of how future wars might be carried out – in other words, where does the responsibility for agency (action) ultimately lie?

There is not much division between the mercenary and the vigilante when it comes to the question of legitimacy and narrative. In the case of a vigilante, as in *Death Wish*, there is a self-made 'social contract' that legitimates their acts of destablisation and revenge – taking on 'the system' and the criminals themselves. If, as these films suggest, the vigilante might be seen to have socially legitimating aspects rooted in contemporary urban dysfunction, then it might also be fair to observe that the existence and operation of private military is a natural consequence of the nature of the modern state. Kyle Ballard makes precisely this argument in assessing the history of private military firms. Endorsing the reading of the modern political state as a corporate entity, Ballard positions the operations of private

military within the demesne of economies of efficiency and consultant spe-
cialisation. He does warn that the wholesale endorsement of mercenary
deployment has risks for political will, stating that a lack of will to 'engage
crises of relatively low consequence' (2007: 39) (to clients) can lead to the
ignoring of human rights abuses and political corruption in low priority
areas (he cites Rwanda as an example; see Ballard 2007: 53).

Though there were straightforward war movies made throughout the
1970s, including *Patton* (1970), *Cross of Iron* (1977) and *A Bridge Too Far*
(1977), they were as notably downbeat and reflexive as the latter-day
westerns and, apart from *Patton*, unsuccessful at the box office. There was
nonetheless an identifiable strain of militarism in films of the period, generally dealing not with large scale military operations, but counter-terrorist
actions like the two Entebbe TV movies *Victory at Entebbe* (1976) and *Raid
on Entebbe* (1976), dramatising the raid by Israeli forces on the hijacked
Air France jet in Uganda that same year. At stake in this kind of film is both
the concept of counter-strike itself – righteous (natural) reaction to acts of
terrorism – and the 'surgical strike' in which the focus of action is specific,
local and of determinate duration. In both films a 'team' of commandos
overthrow the hijackers and rescue a 'community' of passengers intertextual with the disaster films of the era.

This type of military engagement proved more palatable to the audience than depictions of large scale historical battles, which simply raised
the issue of 'national mission' in the face of a divided nation. The same is
true of purely fictive counter-terrorist films of the period including *Black
Sunday* (1977) and *Nighthawks* (1981), which as Prince (2009) points out,
differ in their presentation of terrorist characters as figures of national liberation (intertextual with counter-cultural discourse of the period) rather
than vengeful jihadists. The 'Entebbe formula' would be used again later
in the comparatively big-budget Golan/Globus production *The Delta Force*
(1986), detailing the rescue of a planeload of largely Israeli hostages from
Palestinian terrorists, which Prince highlights as being exemplary of the
more modern configuration of terrorism.

The military films of the 1970s and 1980s therefore largely dealt explicitly in illegitimate warfare within the teleology of moral justification centred
on the actions of anti-heroes. Neatly combining the economic imperative
of a war without national mandate and the reality of the geopolitical situation wherein destablisation and covert activity was becoming standard

operating procedure – the new warrior was no longer legitimated by the state but engaged by a figure of authority whom, by happy coincidence, could also turn out to be morally in the wrong and justly punished by the people he had hired. This allowed these films to again have it both ways. It legitimates military endeavour but disapproves of it in the same gesture.

We see this in *The Wild Geese* (1978) and *The Dogs of War* (1980), where the shady businessmen who hire the mercenaries are ultimately the object of righteous vengeance. Both films involve the deployment of private military organisations by capitalist enterprises nominally acting in the interests of political change. In *The Wild Geese* the specific task is an operation to liberate a metaphoric Nelson Mandela called Julius Limbani (Winston Ntshona), undertaken by a team of mercenaries led by British Colonel Allen Faulkner (Richard Burton). The true agenda behind the mission is the negotiations for commercial interests in the region by contractor Sir Edward Matherson (Stewart Granger). When Matherson successfully concludes negotiations with the ruling regime, he abandons Limbani and the mercenary team. After sustaining heavy losses, including Faulkner's best friend Captain Rafer Janders (Richard Harris), whom Faulker himself has had to shoot to save him from being butchered by government troops armed with machetes, Faulkner manages to return home and kills Matherson. The political becomes personal, in the classic trajectory of this cinema of action.

The Dogs of War is a curious reversal of the dynamics of the previous film in that the capitalist agenda is overt from the beginning as American mercenary Jamie Shannon (Christopher Walken) is engaged by a businessman named Endean (Hugh Miallis) to first scout then overthrow a fictive African nation with platinum mines. In the course of the film Shannon is captured and tortured (an important motif in action films, one we will discuss in the next chapter) and only then encounters a former freedom fighter named Dr Okoye (Winston Ntshona again). When Shannon eventually carries out the coup, he turns control of the country over to Okoye, leaving Endean with the remark that he will have to pay for the country all over again if he wants it.

The Wild Geese and *The Dogs of War* both displace racial issues within white Western societies onto Africa, both making clear that an imperialist and capitalist agenda underlines nominally political acts. The question of 'priorities' that these films raise actually cut directly to anxieties around the neo-imperialism of the period, and though later films would largely unproblematically celebrate these kinds of interventions, here in the 1970s there is still some skepticism, if not downright cynicism. Also, in terms not unlike those suggested in approaching *Straw Dogs*, there is a question of rural displacement in these films, evoking an exotic, 'untamed' landscape in which western and war genres combine to represent military engagement with moral and ethical quagmires peppering the vista.

It is again not much of a stretch to see here a refiguration of questions of the historical relationship between military conquest and law and order with ideas of 'nation' debated previously in both western and war films, now found not just disguised as metaphoric adaptation, but refiguration with regard to contemporary realities, and it is this which underlies the *Rambo* controversy of 1985, with its wish-fulfillment fantasy and the live moral issues that explode around it. Indeed we can locate *Uncommon Valor* and *Missing in Action* directly between these darker-hued morality plays and *Rambo: First Blood Part II*, and likewise see the combination of sombre melancholy and hard-core action in *First Blood* as the bridge between the introspective action drama of the 1970s and the more extrovert and hysterical classical action film of the 1980s, as we shall see in the next chapter.

Driving Form: The Aesthetic of Momentum

At issue in the development of film style and aesthetics in the action films of the 1970s is that as technology evolved and as the 'realist' methodology of the New Hollywood era held sway, the logistics and representation of action became increasingly complex and dangerous. Realistic car chases eschewing back projection in favour of authentic, destructive presentations of vehicular action began with the spectacular ten-minute set piece featuring real driving by Steve McQueen at the heart of *Bullitt*, and soon became a staple of many films both within the category of action/adventure and within more traditional crime films and thrillers like *The French Connection* and *The Seven-Ups* (1973). In aesthetic terms, the action film began to show signs of stylistic formalisation through narratives of pursuit. Dynamic 'action scenes' were gradually becoming not set pieces but the constitutive experience of the films and the means of their sensual and kinesthetic register.

This has roots in the very beginnings of cinema itself when both film-makers and audiences developed a sense of spatial and temporal relationships and continuity editing through simple visual narratives in which characters chased other characters (often cops chasing criminals). The repetitions of shots of spaces with different figures moving through them cut to suggest variances in time established the cinematographic principles upon which continuity editing would be based. It was a slow process, and become more refined and developed into the parallel editing system now taken utterly for granted. But in comprehension terms, those comic and dramatic chase films, with their patterns of repetition and sense of diagetic space, were vital in making action visually legible (see Elsaesser 1990; Grieveson & Krämer 2004; Popple & Kember 2004).

Legibility continues to be a central issue in discussion of the aesthetics of action and spectacle in action movies, with the films of Michael Bay and Tony Scott a traditional target for criticism. Bordwell explores this as what he calls 'intensified continuity' (2002: 16) arguing that rapidity of action is not so much the issue as the readability of sequences, especially as contemporary films increasingly eschew establishing and interlinking shots and overlap dialogue with unrelated action, requiring audiences to 'read ahead' in order to comprehend the sequence. Most interestingly, he suggests that

> The style aims to generate a keen moment-by-moment anticipation. Techniques which 1940s directors reserved for moments of shock and suspense are the stuff of normal scenes today. Close-ups and singles make the shots very legible. Rapid editing obliges the viewer to assemble discrete pieces of information, and it sets a commanding pace: look away and you might miss a key point. In the alternating close views, in the racking focus and the edgily drifting camera, the viewer is promised something significant, or at least new, at each instant. Television-friendly, the style tries to rivet the viewer to the screen. (2002: 24)

This observation resonates with the concept of action in action as outlined by Lichtenfeld (2007) and examined in the introduction. The action film must be alive in the moment for the audience to experience a kinesthetic effect. Bordwell's 'moment-by-moment anticipation' is a good description of the same thing. However, here we have the natural corollary to that as, as Bordwell remarks, the scenes must also be legible.

Car chase films represent the fusion of mind and machine in which the will becomes manifest through mechanisation. The cars became 'characters' and those who drive them are interlinked with their vehicles relative to narrative momentum, emotional expression and agency of action. This is seen in films like *Bullitt* and *The Driver*, reaching something of an apex with *Mad Max 2*. John Orr writes about the automobile as what he terms a 'commodified demon' (1993: 127), arguing that the unmistakable psychoanalytic connection between phallic empowerment and automobile ownership and/or control drives the symbolic substructure of numerous films, ranging from conscious European art-house meditations on car culture such as *Week-End* (1967) to action films featuring car chases.

Tico Romao observes that this function also has its roots in the cultural and economic placement of the automobile in American culture, particularly youth culture of the late 1960s and early 1970s. Here the allure of ownership of a car played into the post-counterculture commercialisation of the ideal of independence, reinforcing the illusion of revolution sustained by the fantasy of volition. Referring to the opening image of *The Cannonball Run* (1981) (itself a derivation of earlier similar films inspired by a real-life illegal road race including *The Gumball Rally* (1976) and *Cannonball* (1976)) in which a speed limit sign is vandalised by one of the participants in an illegal cross country road race, he remarks: 'At the close of the decade, defiance towards highway statutes was seen as a more viable and non-politicized means of representing vehicular lawlessness, a gesture stripped of any true countercultural significance' (2004: 142).

That said, the 'Southern Exploitation' sub-genre was an important site for car chase sequences. Fusion between images of defiance and the freedom provided by vehicular movement across state lines and legal boundaries on the American roadways was the mainstay of *Smokey and the Bandit* and its sequels, but also precursors like the seminal *White Lightning* and its sequel *Gator* (1976), which fit within the category of vigilante and avenger films in thematic and narrative terms. In *White Lightning* a vengeful ex-con helps the authorities to break a moonshine ring run by a corrupt sheriff, climaxing with a lengthy pursuit sequence in which the rural landscape becomes an obstacle course for vehicular navigation and the car itself a tool of justice. As with combat in martial arts, the very duration of the car chase makes the focus on it vital in the experience of action in action. The more comic sequel follows a similar trajectory, with a corrupt politican the target of vehicular vengeance.

The most famous chase sequence of all, to which Orr also refers, is in *Bullitt*. This is, by no-coincidence, a rogue cop film. It depicts the struggles of a police officer who does not trust political authority. Bullitt (McQueen) is a San Francisco police detective engaged to protect a federal witness in a mob trial who finds layers of political expedience between him and his ability to do his job. The film's nominal antagonist is politician Walter Chalmers (Robert Vaughan), more concerned with the appearance of responsibility and attribution of blame than with justice itself. Though the mob are a problem, they are the 'day job' for Bullitt. Political interference represents the intrusion of a social stratum to which he has no access and for which he has no time. Bullitt is clearly disconnected from those around him. He is shown to be so action-driven, so task-focused as to be virtually psychotic: barely sustaining human relationships with his partner Delgetti (Don Gordon) or girlfriend Cathy (the briefly glimpsed Jacqueline Bisset). He even explains himself to the latter that having been exposed to a life of brutality, he is afraid that he is incapable of close relationships.

Bullitt represents a significant change in mode of address from crime films with which it is contemporaneous, such as *Madigan* (1968) or *The Detective* (1968). Though both these films deal with rogue cops (the hero of the latter, Joe Leland, would feature in a 1979 sequel novel entitled *Nothing Lasts Forever*, later adapted into *Die Hard*) and evince both frustration with bureaucracy, *Bullitt* evinces considerably more sophisticated visual language. Where Don Siegel (*Madigan*) and Gordon Douglas (*The Detective*) block and shoot their films with patient attention to classical form, *Bullitt* director Peter Yates and director of photography William A. Fraker pursue their leading man throughout the film with the gaze of an aroused voyeur. The camera tracks and moves around McQueen's face and body as if kept in orbit by a magnetic field. McQueen's body in space is rendered with less interest in that space than Siegel shows in *Coogan's Bluff* or *Dirty Harry*, but does, as a consequence, far more significantly emphasise the movement of that body in that space.

From its opening scene during which the camera rarely remains static, the film is constantly in motion. This applies to both what's on the screen and how it has been put there. Whenever there is a scene of relative quiet, it is in anticipation of explosive action, be it hit men bursting in to assassinate the witness to moments of domestic isolation. The aesthetic mirrors the hero's restless discomfort with the world around him. The viewer is given the sense that Bullitt is never wholly comfortable unless he is in command and in motion. A similar aesthetic was deployed ironically by John Boorman in *Point Blank* (1967) just one year earlier, where the anti-hero's illusion of command is at issue – he seems in control (and the camera tracks his movement), but never actually is because he is a brutish anachronism in an evolving modern criminal world. Even his name, 'Walker' is a marker – he walks while everyone else drives.

In *Bullitt*, it is command of motorised transport that ultimately roots its hero in the modern frame. The film's famous central car chase is dynamically shot with real vehicles in genuine locations and with McQueen actually driving his car for the most part. This is significant in itself, as it fuses the audience's sense of Bullitt's world with the image of McQueen driving his 1968 Ford Mustang GT. It is a marker of the new cinematic aesthetic, devoid of backdrop or stunt doubles; here is a film of action about a man of action in which a man really is in action.

In the key sequence Bullitt is pursued by mobsters who intend to kill him. As he drives, a series of rapid intercuts of him inside the car driving, the exterior of the car as he moves, and images of his eyes in his car mirrors as he observes the world create a sense of tension and unease. Bullitt realises he is being pursued and so vanishes from their sight. This reverses the anxiety. His would-be pursuers now urgently scan their surroundings. Then the Mustang appears in their rear view mirror: the hunted has become the hunter. The chase ensues out of San Francisco and onto the Pacific Highways, where vehicular collision, gunplay and constant forward momentum constitute the entirety of the action. There is no dialogue, no explanation, no commentary – just a chase and combat scene ending in the destruction of the mobsters' car in a crash and explosion. The spectacle of vehicular chase and combat could easily be described as erotically charged, and certainly provides the template for developments later in the decade where the fetishism of the motor vehicle reaches new extremes.

This would be extended in films including *Vanishing Point* (1971), *Two-Lane Blacktop* and *The Driver,* developed to the point of mysticism. *The Driver* consciously connects the car chase with the mythic western hunter/outlaw motif in refusing even to give its characters names. Pursing detective Bruce Dern refers to his quarry, Ryan O'Neal, as 'cowboy', and the taciturn title character expresses himself primarily through his coolness and expertise in control of a vehicle. This is an image that would repeat itself many times throughout this era and thereafter, contributing to a sense that an action cinema was in constant motion, narratively, textually, thematically and aesthetically because it was literally driven. The trajectory in *Vanishing Point* is towards nihilism. Kowalski (Barry Newman) deliberately rams his car into a bulldozer at the film's climax in full view of the crowd of supporters he has gathered in the course of his odyssey. *Two-Lane Blacktop* is, if anything, even more oblique, and features an even greater number of point-of-view shots and less dialogue. Director Monte Hellman (who had directed westerns) would even remark in an interview that the deployment of vehicles and the image of the road, so quickly and easily read as American identity and a sense of search and journey were 'a cultural appendage ... side effects' (see Walker 1971: 37).

Though we can see therefore that the car chase becomes something of a marker for the more universal aesethic shift in the presentation of action, the car chase also becomes an identifiable sub-genre, rooted in a particular configuration of volition in the teleological context of mechanisation and alienation. It would reach something of an apex with the Australian-produced *Mad Max* series. *Mad Max* (1979) in particular seemed to be something of a *ne plus ultra*, with an early scene depicting a psychotic villain called 'The Night Rider' (Vince Gill) helpfully summarising the spirit of things by screaming 'I am the Night Rider, a fuel-injected suicide machine!' The psychic fusion of man and machine is best exemplified cinematically in the climactic scene where ex-cop Max Rockatansky (Mel Gibson) figuratively *becomes* his car. The scene marks the end of Max's attempt to maintain his hold on sanity and social order following the death of his partner and the murders of his wife and child at the hands of a ruthless biker gang. Furious ('mad') and determined to avenge himself on the bikers, Max walks away from the camera at the centre of the widescreen frame into a darkened parking garage. Seconds later, his vehicle roars directly towards the camera from the same darkness. Max and machine are one; bent on destruction and revenge. It is a simple, elegant image, but one that resonates with the symbolic function of the car in the action movie throughout this decade. However, the film concludes with an image of the unending highway – the empty road down which Max must now travel. His actions

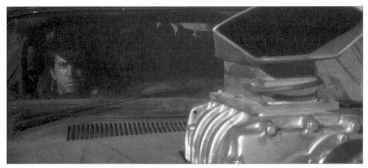

Man and machine: Mel Gibson faces apocalypse from his car in *Mad Max 2* (1981)

have brought him transcendence and vengeance, but not restoration.

Mad Max 2 begins with a situation of absolute desolation following the complete collapse of civilisation. This amplification of the moral wasteland of the colonialist mercenary movie provides a more obvious metaphor for cultural displacement than merely geographical transference by shifting to a post-apocalyptic desert (which, by no small coincidence, also resembles the landscape of the western). Imagery of social collapse had already been featured in previous car chase films like *Death Race 2000* (1975) in which a murderous road race is the entertainment of the future, and *Damnation Alley* (1977) in which a heavily modified vehicle attempts to cross a nuclear wasteland on a mission of mercy. Even less fantastical car films like *Gone in 60 Seconds* (1974) and its sequel *The Junkman* (1982), or *The Blues Brothers* (1980) were arguably somewhat apocalyptic. The orgiastic and largely meaningless destruction of real vehicles certainly seemed to some critics to suggest a collapse of rationality of a kind.

Mad Max 2 is set in a world where natural resources have all but run out and gangs of marauders roam the wastelands in customised vehicles. Max, still on the road seemingly since the events of the first film, encounters a group of settlers besieged by such marauders. He offers to help the settlers for the price of his continued freedom. He therefore stands in the middle of Manichean divisions of civilised and uncivilised, neatly fusing the multiple roles of action anti-heroes of the era – cop, mercenary, vigilante avenger and car driver operating in a 'new West' in which social crisis has resulted in collapse, and the only feasible reaction is restoration through movement.

The film is a virtual textbook on the filming of vehicular momentum, with dramatic stuntwork and an evocation of high-speed pursuit reminiscent of the great western stagecoach chase scenes, but now highly mechanised. The film is highlighted by the sustained chase scene that comprises the entire third act in which Max upscales from a car to a fuel truck, drawing the attentions of vicious wasteland raiders in customised cars and outfits determined to stop him and steal his cargo.

Mick Broderick locates the *Mad Max* trilogy within the rubric of cinematic apocalypticism coinciding with postmodernist discourse on the collapse of capitalism. He argues that the series' Judeo-Christian messianic bent is significant in locating the film where 'we can readily observe a consistency in their developing narrative ideology, one which overtly conforms to pre-existing apocalyptic metatexts of social legitimization, yet may simultaneously deflate this via an ironic artistic strategy of bricolage' (1993: 267). This reading certainly corresponds with the placement of these and other action films within the framework of a reactive philosophy, though Broderick's suggestion that the film's aesthetic is ironic may be overly reductive of its absolute commitment to an visual register both of movement and destruction.

David Chute observes of director George Miller's visual interests, 'he puts some kind of stimulating spin on every object, character, and incident he invents' (1982: 28), a detail which calls to mind Bordwell's conception of imagistic detail as focusing strategy rather than an undercutting of its own visual texture. However, as the action intensifies, the film literally strips away most of its bricolage like layers of clothing or vehicular modification. As the heavily-armed, heavily-customised raiders are driven off one by one, the truck becomes a stripped-down fast-moving mythic icon of forward momentum. In this it is reminiscent of the demon truck of *Duel* (1971), which may have inspired it. Spielberg's earlier film certainly at least provides a precedent for both the exclusion of excess meaning and the logistics of filming relentless vehicular action.

In narrative terms this hurtling truck, this icon of momentum and agency, is actually a symbolic misdirection. The settlers who have hired Max have filled it with sand, not fuel. When it finally comes to a halt, spilling its cargo, Max seems genuinely surprised by this, although also amused. This makes Max, like his counterparts in *The Dogs of War* and *The Wild Geese*, betrayed. It is clearly indicated, however, that this 'betrayal' enables salvation – the settlers escape. At the end of the film, it is Max who has ceased to be in motion. Our final image of him is of a figure standing framed by the skyline, staring towards the camera while the voice of the narrator (revealed to be the 'feral child' who has been his sidekick throughout the film) explains that the settlers found their way to safety – in other words they, not Max, are on the road.

This comes full circle in *Mad Max Beyond Thunderdome* (1985) where he becomes an icon of redemption for a tribe of lost children by leading them away from the ersatz 'civilisation' of Bartertown, defined by exploitation and conflict, and inspiring their journey to their mythic 'tomorrow-morrow land'. Of this third film Lichtenfeld observes that the construction of the wilderness to which Max restores tradition, ritual and even myth is nothing less than a distillation of the mythology of the American action film: 'These are the myths of the frontier hero who rescues and renews, and of the savage enemy who can be found at the business end of the hero's weapons (primal and otherwise) or, at the very least, of his steely reserve' (2007: 158).

Throughout this chapter we have seen this 'steely reserve' raised in the face of a considerable and ever-mounting sense of crisis, disaster and even apocalypse: a response which is rarely renewing, though that is often the intent. That said the apocalypticism of the *Mad Max* films does in an important way cap the era of the war at home in the action movie, literally presenting a *tablua rasa* of a society destroyed rather than a complex one in a state of flux or change through which the anti-hero must navigate physically and morally. This image cannot but resonate with the broader image of social failure which hangs over this entire period and against which the action film must be seen to present nothing short of a desperate and despairing reaction.

2 THE HYPERBOLIC BODY

Tests of Strength

In *First Blood* Vietnam veteran John Rambo (Sylvester Stallone) visits a small town in the Pacific Northwest in search of an old war buddy, only to find the man has died. Rambo runs afoul of the local Sheriff, Will Teasle (Brian Dennehy), who arrests him after he refuses to leave town. The latter part of the story is well known. Enraged, Rambo runs wild in the surrounding mountains and later the town itself, deploying his guerrilla skills first against Teasle and his deputies, then State Troopers and the National Guard, who bring in his former commander Colonel Trautman (Richard Crenna) to talk him down. But what is it that enrages Rambo so? What is the inciting incident that sparks the violent reaction?

It comes when Rambo is being processed by Teasle's deputies. Deputy Sergeant Galt (Jack Starrett) strikes Rambo in the back, then, as another deputy approaches with a razor to shave him, Galt uses his baton to trap Rambo's arms. This triggers a gruesome flashback of Rambo crucified in a bamboo cage then having his chest sliced by a Vietnamese soldier. Rambo snaps, reliving the trauma by dint of visual (or perhaps, in his case, kinesthetic) associations between being restrained with the baton and his crucifixion, and between the knife and the razor, and he responds with the instinct to escape. He battles his way out of the station, steals a motorbike and makes for the hills. It is an act of flight, but soon becomes a fight. The poster advertising for the film played on Stallone's association with *Rocky*

(1976) with the evocation of the word 'fight': 'This time he's fighting for his life' it claimed.

The action which follows, making up the bulk of the film, is a series of interconnected sequences depicting, first, Rambo's attempt to survive and evade pursuit, then his sustained resistance as he 'takes the fight to them' guerilla style – restaging Vietnam in North America – then finally his revenge after Rambo is left for dead following the deliberate collapse of a mine where he has been hiding. The containment proves illusory and Rambo emerges from the sewers into the town, where he works his way towards Teasle. The film is elemental in its depiction of this phased battle – from the open-air mountain town with which it begins to increasingly enclosed scenes of rain-soaked forest to the muddy flooded mine where fire burns to the night assault on the town where explosions and gunfire shatter the peace of rural Americana. Rambo is comparatively non-verbal once the 'fight' begins. His actions are focused on his combat skillset. He improvises weapons, shelter and traps. Though he picks off his pursuers, he is hunted by men, dogs and even helicopters – a body driven, chased, hounded, 'pushed' beyond endurance. His fight back only begins after he is presumed dead and like the proverbial return of the repressed, he emerges to bring trauma to those who have traumatised him.

In his study of trauma in cinema Kirby Farrell applies the terminology and clinical definitions of injury and stress under four headings that are 'useful for thinking about culture' (1998: 11), namely: the long-term influence of injury after initial shock; the tendency towards dissociation (which he defines in terms of a loss of control – a screening out of unconfrontable pain); the contagiousness of post-traumatic stress; and the destabilisation of conventional reality and the arousal of death anxiety. All of these aptly describe the process and conditions behind the evolution of the action film into a coherent mode of discourse. It should be noted in observing this that there is no suggestion of, as Prince (2009) warns, conflating cultural and personal memory on a proximate, experiential level – films do not induce trauma, though they may reflect it like a kind of social memory. He cites Marita Sturken, who speaks of 'prosthetic memories' (1997: 11) that circulate because of audiences' cultural engagement with technologies like cinema. Action movies literally embody injury and trauma, representing its effects and projecting cathartic volition in acts of response and restoration.

The embodiment of 'long term influence' can be seen in the persist-ence of social trauma as subject and as sub-text. Žižek is careful to make a distinction between trauma as experienced in the West (short, sharp acts of violation and terror) and enduring trauma such as in Sudan or the Congo. He says of the latter: 'It is almost an oxymoron to refer to them as "post-traumatic" subjects, since what makes their situation so traumatic is the very *persistence* of trauma' (2010: 293). This division is suggestive of the reactive frameworks of (Western) action cinema as distinct from articulations of persistent psychic trauma. Yet Farrell makes the point that the condition known as Post Traumatic Stress Disorder (PTSD) was itself the locus of political agitation as veterans fought for clinical recognition of the disorder through its proposed inclusion in the American Psychiatric Association's *Diagnostic and Statistical Manual of Mental Disorders* as part of an ongoing campaign for legal recourse for veterans in trouble with the Law (see Farrell 1998: 11). This enduring trauma, manifesting itself beyond the immediate shock of experience and resonating broadly throughout politics and society, would find a new cultural locus in the 1980s begin-ning with *First Blood*.

First Blood is clearly a 1970s trauma narrative, based on the 1972 novel by David Morrell. The film would not have been out of place if released during that decade. Rambo would then have represented another one of the many socially disenfranchised 'crazed vets' that served as a symbol of larger sociopolitical problems in films like *Dog Day Afternoon* (1975) and *Taxi Driver* (1976), not least of all in that in the novel Rambo dies. He is shot in the back of the head with a shotgun by Trautman – society's problem 'solved' by the destruction of the Frankenstein monster by its own crea-tor. The film is also a trauma narrative, but one which offers redemption. Rambo lives, for one thing, but in living he represents the possibility of salvation and 'cure' for the post-traumatic malady. Rambo is embraced by Trautman; invited back from the brink of apocalypse to join civilisation, albeit in prison. It offers this resolution because the film was made in an era already being demarcated with narratives of hope and uplift cor-responding with the so-called 'Reagan Revolution'.

Susan Jeffords examines the correlations between the ideology of the 'Reagan Revolution' and the cinema of the period. Linking Reagan's calcu-lated persona and experience as an actor with the idea of a political imagi-nation, she demonstrates how the broad rhetorical statement had a way of becoming a *de facto* political reality, not least of all in the willingness of American cinema to embrace this image of a new cultural confidence. She notes that narratives 'of heroism, success, achievement, toughness, strength, and "good old Americanness"' (1994: 15) that predominated were reflective of the cultural and political shift which Reagan's speeches and public image evoked. The point, she explains, is not whether or not Reagan 'caused' these things, but that in consciously representing an image of America and its Presidency in direct and deliberate contrast to that of Presidents before him, Reagan was both positing and embodying a sense of national identity that resonated across popular culture. The Reagan years were to be, in every way, a restoration of confidence and a renewal of self in the face of a traumatic past that was not to be erased, but refigured.

Farrell's dissociative 'screening out' of unconfrontable pain is also seen in this redemption – a re-envisioning of historical trauma as symbolic victory, soon applied across a range of themes and subjects surrounding general racial, class and family/gender issues sometimes apart from (*Die Hard*) and sometimes related to (*Lethal Weapon*) a Vietnam experience. It was also often seen in the displacement of Cold War anxiety onto narratives of direct confrontation with what Reagan himself had termed the 'Evil Empire' – the Soviet Union. This is seen in films including *Red Dawn* (1984) where a group of high school students battle Soviet and Cuban forces that have taken over their hometown, *Invasion USA* (1985) where Chuck Norris does much the same thing on his own, and *Rambo III* (1988) in which Rambo enters Soviet-controlled Afghanistan and instigates revolution.

The aspect of 'contagion' to which Farrell refers is evident in the genre's industrial consolidation. With the rise of the Cannon Group and Joel Silver at arguably opposite ends of the economic scale as producers of identifiable genre product, action films became recognised and anticipated by audiences. Jennifer Bean argues that the cinema provided what she terms 'trauma thrills' (2004: 17) – embodying the shock of modernity and the sociological, psychological and emotional trauma of change in a type of bodily experience (watching films) that is orchestrated to delimit the effect and make it pleasurable. This, naturally enough, also makes these pleasures marketable, and this is precisely what we see in the wholesale production of sequels, series and low-budget imitations of successful big-budget films that constitute genre production. This can be seen in the profusion of films starring Chuck Norris, Michael Dudikoff, Jean-Claude Van Damme and Steven Seagal offering variants on the formulae of major studio films with Mel Gibson, Bruce Willis, Sylvester Stallone and Arnold Schwarzenegger. Prince (2009) also puts this in the context of anti-Palestinian terrorist narratives emerging following the upsurge in political violence in the early 1980s, citing the Israeli Cannon Group as a particular locus of this corpus of work.

Farrell's fourth characteristic of trauma – the destablisation of reality and arousal of death anxiety – is, in fact, a defining feature of the cinema of action – 'This time he's fighting for his life.' The threat of 'death' hung over society itself in the 1970s action film, and arguably represented an existential impulse to self-destruction. Throughout the 1980s, again the threat of death is evident, but its locus tends to be not so much society as the actual body. The body is threatened with death, yes, but also injury, torture and trial. Importantly though, the body is also the site at which this trauma can be overcome by strength of will.

Jeffords equates the 'hard body' of the action hero era with the re-masculinsation of America (as a world power) and American men (whose self-image had undergone the trauma of the struggles for racial and sexual equality in the preceding decades). Yvonne Tasker (1993) points out that in doing so these films were merely refiguring what had gone before, but she is interested in the way that popular culture reaffirms preexisting stereotypes and myths, and reiterates that it centres them ultimately on the body in racial and sexual modes.

It should be borne in mind though that not all bodies are equal, not even within the dominant 'white male' bracket. There is a qualitative difference in musculature between the hyperbolic, bemuscled Stallone and Schwarzenegger body and the leaner, more agile Chuck Norris, Jean-Claude Van Damme or Steven Seagal variety, let alone the visibly aging, more 'traditional' (and arguably 'western') body of Charles Bronson and Clint Eastwood. Variances at this level relate back to Anderson's (1998) conception of the body in motion, and the visualisation of that body in action. Though narrative and theme unite the avenger films of Bronson and Eastwood (both reprising their 1970s characters and variations on them throughout the era), Norris, Van Damme and Seagal (emerging from martial arts backgrounds), and Stallone and Schwarzenegger (emphasising musculature), their visual pleasures (and level of spectacle and display) are different. Where they do not differ is their conception of a hero in action – undergoing trials of various kinds, frequently tortures, in order to overcome a challenge to their values.

In *Rambo: First Blood Part II* Rambo undergoes torture at the hands of the Soviet allies of the Vietnamese forces who are still holding American prisoners ten years after the end of the Vietnam War. After being captured and immersed in a slime pit, he is taken to a room in the prison compound and tied to a metal bedframe attached to an electrical generator. In a sustained sequence intercutting Rambo writhing in agony as current runs through his body with the awestruck reactions of prisoners and guards alike as the lights in the compound dim with every charge, the audience is invited to 'feel his pain'. Editing intensifies the audience's sense of Rambo's experience, deploying a montage of details of his reactions to the pain (a grimace, a scream, a turn of the head) while being electrocuted, then cutting to more static medium-shots between jolts. Making it all worse in narrative terms is the fact that Rambo has been caught only because he has been betrayed. Sent in by the CIA to photograph an empty prison camp and satisfy political curiosity at home, Rambo has found actual POWs and attempted to liberate them. When Rambo's CIA handler, Marshall Murdock (Charles Napier), is informed by the evacuation team that Rambo has a live prisoner, he orders them to abandon him.

Rambo is being tortured in an effort to obtain his collusion. The Soviet officer, Colonel Podovksy (Steven Berkoff), wants Rambo to make a propaganda broadcast condemning the American government, which under the circumstances might not seem unreasonable from Rambo's point of view. But Rambo does not break. His body convulses under restraint. Sweat pours from his face. He even screams. But when Podovsky orders one of his men to shove a heated knife into the eye of the very POW Rambo was trying to escape with, Rambo gives in. He is given a microphone and shortwave radio with which to contact his HQ. He struggles to the table and makes the necessary adjustments to the frequency and makes contact. Peals of thunder are heard. A storm is brewing. There is anticipation here: anxiety. The audience has just registered a scene of seemingly unendurable physical trauma and knows in narrative terms that this is a double betrayal for the protagonist of *First Blood*. How will his trauma manifest itself? How will he react?

This torture scene is one of the few moments where the 'action' in this film halts. The film on the whole is, like its predecessor, virtually

an assemblage of scenes of precise physical action of mounting intensity – beginning with the explosion at the rock quarry which opens the
film and following Rambo through his preparation (featuring the genre's
now-characteristic 'suiting up' montage), travel (disastrous – he loses the
equipment because his diving rig does not disengage from the jet), recon-
naissance (moving swiftly through the jungle avoiding detection and meeting his Vietnamese confederate Co Bao (Julia Nickson-Soul)), and finally
the aborted rescue. The film depicts the momentum of survival, defense
and revenge alternating scenes of evasion, flight and pursuit with scenes
of combat, crisply photographed with elements within the frame including
buffeting winds, helicopter blades, burning fires, churning waters and bil-
lowing smoke, all moving at all times.

The torture scene, by contrast, is dialogue heavy. Podovksy's interrogation and cajoling verbally contextualises Rambo's physical ordeal. Tasker
notes the prevalence of punishment in these films, where the hero's body
is not a necessarily a site of self-evident strength. She observes 'suffering,
and torture in particular, operates as both a set of narrative hurdles to
be overcome (tests the hero must survive) and as a set of aestheticised
images to be lovingly dwelt on' (1993: 125). This aptly describes this particular sequence. It also summarises the trope of the torture scene in general
terms. Sometimes the torture isn't literal as it is here or in *Lethal Weapon*,
but a more generalised beating received by the hero where he is beaten up,
bested, overwhelmed and 'put down'. This happens frequently, as far back
as *Dirty Harry* and *Walking Tall*. It usually marks a classical screenwriting
'belly of the whale' moment where the hero is at his lowest ebb and at
seemingly the most unendurable apex of his body trauma. The cinematic
and narrative pause represented by this particular 'test of strength' triggers
the third-act reversal where the hero moves from resistance to revenge.
It also builds anticipation on the audience's part for precisely that – the
counter-attack, the reprisal – action as (justifiable) *reaction*.

This is exactly what happens here, as Rambo moves from stealth
(survival) and capture (resistance) to combat (revenge). After his torture,
Rambo's contact with the base is terse. Glancing around him in the room,
he sees through the floorboard that his ally Co is hiding underneath the
raised floor and is armed. He grips the microphone stand tightly with one
hand and says only 'Murdock'. When Murdock comes on the line and deliv-
ers platitudes about coming to get him, a sequence of close-up shots of the

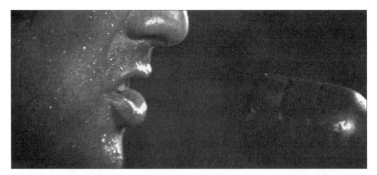

'I'm coming to get *you*': Stallone promises vengeance in *Rambo: First Blood Part II* (1985)

assembled and equally anxious cast of characters delays the action. The film cuts from Rambo to Podovksy, to the torturer (Vojo Goric), to Colonel Trautman at base, and to Murdock, each image sustained enough to register each character's sense of anticipation and give the audience more time to share it. 'Murdock', repeats Rambo. Thunder. Lightning illuminating half of Rambo's sweat-drenched face. He grips the microphone stand again, even more tightly. His knuckles are heard cracking. We cut to a profile of Rambo's face, which is just Stallone's mouth, chin and characteristically curved semi-paralysed lips. Says Rambo 'I'm coming to get *you*.' We see Murdock's face, registering fear. Chaos ensues. We cut back to the camp, where Rambo uses the microphone to knock the Russians unconscious while Co fires through the floor. Rambo escapes. His mission is now not only rescue and redemption, but revenge.

The final twenty minutes of the film consists of an ever-mounting series of violent confrontations between Rambo and enemy military, moving from the use of his knife and bow and arrow (with explosive tips) to battles against helicopters of increasing size and ferocity, including the enormous Soviet gunship piloted by Podovsky which Rambo destroys with a grenade launcher. The act concludes with Rambo's arrival at base where he finally confronts Murdock. After a clearly cathartic moment where Rambo uses the unfeasibly large M60 machine gun he has taken from a helicopter mounting frame to destroy the paraphernalia of bureaucratic control – the command centre computer system – he approaches Murdock with evident menace, drawing his combat knife. But, in yet another reversal, he slams the knife into Murdock's desk saying 'Mission accomplished', then admonishes him to seek out the other POWs that the government knows are out there: 'Find 'em' he says, 'or I'll find you.' The body has endured its trials, overcome its traumas, and now confronts society with its demand for change, restoration and redemption.

I Got Your Back: Bodies and Buddies

In *American Ninja* (1985) soldier Joe Armstrong (Michael Dudikoff) finds himself at odds with other members of the US Army at a base in the Philippines when he alone survives a Ninja attack. Armstrong is a blow-in, a conscript evading jail and also armed with martial arts training signalling his 'difference'. In a key scene about half an hour into the film Armstrong proves his worthiness when he defeats respected Corporal Curtis Jackson (Steve James) in single combat. Jackson is a martial arts instructor with a commanding presence. He bears a toned-down version of the blaxploitation look – moustache, big(ish) hair and street lingo including words like 'baby' and 'man'. Armstrong (the name doesn't even demand comment) defeats Jackson by using primarily defensive moves, repeatedly throwing him to the ground but never striking. Finally when another solider gives Jackson a short pole with which to best the evasive Armstrong, the latter puts a bucket on his head and invites Jackson to hit him. Armstrong evades the blow even though he cannot see, disarms Jackson, throws him to the ground again and makes to strike with the pole, but halts hovering over his face, indicating he could have hit if he wanted to. Jackson admits defeat and announces it to the assembled men. He then sides with Armstrong when a military superior arrives, claiming it was a demonstration. When Jackson asks Armstrong where he learned 'his moves', Armstrong tells him he has picked them up 'on the streets'. Jackson doesn't believe him: 'I'm from the streets', he says.

The explicit hand-over of the role of black action hero to white in this scene makes transparent the interracial dynamics of the action movie. The so-called 'blaxploitation' film of the 1970s was very particular in its construction of concepts of society and action. By focusing on a confined sociopolitical and urban environment the concept of 'action' became localised as a mobilisation of racial and class tensions, often displaced onto a 'ghetto hierarchy' which often led to a white (and corporate, certainly capitalist) villain. The classic crime film's concern with economic mobility and vengeance against the 'haves' by the 'have nots' appealed to a genuinely disenfranchised black community, but also to the more broad urban audience. As Von Doviak (2005) remarked, the Southern Exploitation films constituted a kind of rural white American folklore; so, in spite of itself or perhaps consciously, did blaxploitation serve as an urban folklore, albeit one constructed within the demesne of white, patrimonial modes of representation and industrial film production.

In many ways blaxploitation is the action film in microcosm, a rhetorical counter-strike against the genuine social anxieties that served to fuel public engagement with but also ultimately dismissal of the actual political issues surrounding those anxieties. Cedric Robinson summarises the particulars with reference to blaxploitation, but his words are apt for all action film: 'The cinematic deceit transmuted liberation into vengeance, the pursuit of a social justice which embraced race, class, and gender into black racism, and the politics of armed struggle into systematic assassination' (1998: 6). He points out that the strength and aggression demonstrated by these larger-than-life action heroes drew audiences' line of sight away from the realities of class, race and political struggles and onto simplistic urban avenger fantasies, rupturing the transmission of radical thought.

Inevitably, blaxploitation declined as a popular form, but it left an impact on the action film not least in the sense of a narrative dynamic of righteous aggression against repression. The real trick (and it wasn't that difficult) was to switch the racial profile around so that white characters could become as disenfranchised in narrative terms as their black predecessors were, and in so doing, erase the actual political context of racial prejudice and injustice which was a site of social trauma. Robinson points out, of course, that there was nothing authentic about the representation of the struggle for liberation in blaxploitation, noting, as observed in chapter one with regard to *Death Wish*, that the urban space is a mythical, almost expressionistic staging ground for a philosophy of vengeance, not a locus for political articulation.

The template for the interracial or biracial buddy film long predates the 1980s action movie. It developed from a groundbreaking trope across films including *The Defiant Ones* (1958) and *In the Heat of the Night* (1967), in which white characters gradually bestow respect upon black ones, sometimes forging semi-equal partnerships. This was quickly adopted as a formula in the television series *I Spy* (TV, 1965–68). The show's stars, Robert

Culp and Bill Cosby, re-teamed for the Walter Hill-scripted *Hickey & Boggs* (1972). It was Hill's *48 Hrs.* (1982) that probably most strongly established the interracial buddy film within what would become its dominant mode – a mixture of comic/ironic and action with comedy as its pressure valve and its means of safely dramatising the interracial dynamics of the film.

48 Hrs. begins with a tense and dynamic scene depicting the escape by violent convict Albert Ganz (James Remar) from a chain gang. Its western genre imagery, complete with dusty landscape, hat-wearing guards and pistol- and shotgun-based combat is yet another reminder of Hill's aware-ness of western conventions, following the urban westerns *The Driver* and *The Warriors* (1979) and his actual western *The Long Riders* (1980). The film then moves to San Francisco where bedraggled 'rogue cop' Jack Cates (Nick Nolte) runs afoul of Ganz and his own ethnic henchman Billy Bear (Sonny Landham – in a variant on the stoic Native American he would play in *Predator*) during a shoot-out in which two officers are killed and Cates's gun is stolen. In order to track down Ganz, Cates must enlist the help of Reggie Hammond (Eddie Murphy), formerly part of Ganz's gang and now in prison. Cates effects Hammond's temporary release from incarceration (for 48 hours) and goes on the trail. The tensions of race, class and simply of cops and robbers play out between the two men, first as outright antagonism, gradually developing into a partnership of sorts: 'we ain't brothers, we ain't partners and we ain't friends' growls Cates early on, a line Hammond later repeats back to him with equal venom but which makes the audience laugh because they recognise the irony inherent in the repetition.

48 Hrs. is clearly another white male angst film and a narrative of redemption based on a momentum of action and resolution, but what is interesting in terms of the present discussion is the ways in which the racial dynamic functions. Ed Guerrero (1993) points out the ultimate trajectory of the narrative is towards the continued subordination of the 'buddy', who returns to prison at the end. He also makes the argument that the film's most famous scene, where Hammond comically rousts a redneck bar in an explicit reversal of the ghetto bar-rousting scene in *The French Connection* ultimately suggests white angst at the wielding of black power as stridently as it articulates a turnabout of racial prejudice for comic effect.

Neal King argues that humour is not necessarily supposed to erase racial tension, but 'can air the frustration that racism breeds rather than cover it up (and maybe give embarrassed white guys a vent for their chagrin as they absorb the stinging rebuke)' (1999: 95–6). In this King is not presenting an apologia for racism by way of humorous comic relief, but pointing out that the obviousness of an expression does not necessarily close down its function *in action*. The issue of race and racial conflict is voiced, present and explicit in the film, literally coming to blows as Reggie and Jack, like Armstrong and Jackson, fight in order to establish equality (though Jack gets in the last punch).

Central to the 'buddy' dynamic is the element of transference whereby ideas and values are exchanged through a shared experience. Especially in cop movies, the added professional dynamic of a working partnership also leads to a homosocial bonding and the development of a relationship of trust. Any threat to that relationship becomes, in effect, a threat of schism: an attack on one is an attack on both. This is a matter of structure, not psychology. This effect occurs by the end of *48 Hrs.*, in that the climatic shoot-out, like that of *Beverly Hills Cop* (1984) and *Lethal Weapon* ultimately involves both black and white protagonists firing at the (white, dysfunctional) antagonist. This physical and psychological doubling also frequently provides a vengeance motive in films where the rogue cop's partner is killed, as effectively this amounts to a symbolic death of their own and enables the counter-strike to be 'personal'.

More importantly though is that the legitimating of the white cop's angst comes through his relationship with the black go-between, who, as King points out, 'teaches the white hero how to attend to his lover, maintain loyalties, earn trust, and rethink his racial paranoia' (1999: 93). Throughout the film Hammond has coached Cates on his combative relationships with his superiors and his girlfriend. Though this is usually at least partly comic, the effect is the same. Cates's behaviour changes and he is seen to benefit from Hammond's advice.

As Tasker (1993) points out, the most extreme example of the helper motif is in *Die Hard* where Sergeant Al Powell (Reginald Veljohnson) is re-masculinised by association with John McClane (Bruce Willis), the mythic white male action hero who has been the active agent throughout the film as he battles terrorists inside the high rise Nakatomi building while Powell remains largely static outside. At the end of the film it is Powell who kills Karl (Alexander Godunov), the last terrorist, who was presumed dead but has masqueraded as a hostage and emerges, bloodied, armed and enraged. Powell, desk-bound because of an accident where he shot a child, has never drawn his gun since. He draws it now, following his film-long friendship with McClane, conducted over Powell's police car radio. Re-masculinised by association, he acts at the crucial moment. The counterpoint to this process is the legitimacy which Powell gives to McClane, in that his professional status as a cop is consistently recognised by Powell even when his superiors wonder if McClane is a terrorist in disguise, and also by way of contrast in that Powell's desk-bound bureaucratic life is contrasted with McClane's active, blue collar heroism as a 'frontline' agent of action.

Possibly the most recognised configuration of the buddy dynamic is in the *Lethal Weapon* films, which are also summative of many genre conventions in themselves. In *Lethal Weapon* Martin Riggs (Mel Gibson) is a suicidal Vietnam veteran whose wife has died, leaving him firmly at the fringes of civilisation and a capacity for duty to society. His partnering with older, more experienced family man Roger Murtaugh (Danny Glover) becomes a locus not of racial tension, but of the battle between the death anxiety of the 1970s (coded via Vietnam, which surfaces not only as Riggs' site of personal trauma, but also of the operations of the film's villains, an extortion and profit-oriented mercenary operation formed in Vietnam and ironically named Shadow Company) and the positivity of the affluent Reaganite 1980s of which Murtaugh is a clear beneficiary (nice home, large family, professional profile – success). Riggs is therefore clearly positioned as the disenfranchised in need of integration as well as redemption.

My buddy, my body: Mel Gibson and Danny Glover share a moment in *Lethal Weapon* (1987)

Integration is, inevitably, a term not used lightly given the racial dynamic in the film, but it is accurate.

Across the *Lethal Weapon* films this narrative of integration becomes ever more explicitly focused on family which, from the first film straight through, is the firm centre of a functional and fulfilled society. In *Lethal Weapon 2* (1989) Riggs is reactivated as a figure of heterosexual romance by a relationship with a South African Embassy aide, Rika van den Haas (Patsy Kensit), but she is murdered, providing a doubling of Riggs' trauma in losing his wife. Though the homosocial bonding with Murtaugh has provided these films with a subtext of love, it has been firmly coded within the demesne of heterosexuality by Murtaugh's family status. By *Lethal Weapon 3* (1992) he has become incorporated into Murtaugh's family so fully that it is inevitable that he be presented with the possibility of a (white) family of his own, which is provided by the introduction of detective Lorna Cole (Rene Russo), who matches Riggs in strength and determination. As you might therefore expect, her role by *Lethal Weapon 4* (1998) is to be pregnant, essentially concluding Riggs' journey to full social reactivation with marriage and procreation as the final movement of the film's narrative.

The *Lethal Weapon* films suggest a cumulative narrative of integration and normalisation – a taking back of the place of the white male as the locus of core, settled, 'family' (American, patrimonial) values with the aid of if not necessarily at the expense of a black character. It is significant that this redemption takes place by way of taming an initially suicidal impulse that has made the character into the 'lethal weapon' of the title – an antisocial killing machine: 'Have you ever met anybody you didn't kill?' quips Murtaugh. By the third film any trace of Riggs' 'suicidal' persona has vanished. The self-destructive 'death wish' of the anti-hero has dissolved.

The *Lethal Weapon* films represent the beginning of the end of the 'hard body' hero who is here encoded specifically as psychologically deranged but redeemable, becoming increasingly socially integrated as the series progresses. As Fred Pfeil remarks, it is significant that 'only thanks to the presence and influence of the nurturant, supportive, domestic black buddy can the white hero at last let himself be straightforwardly soft and sensitive too' (1995: 14). Whereas the *Rambo* films posit integration at the expense of political and social expediency – Rambo demands his redemption like a monster from the id – the *Lethal Weapon* films, complete with their

subplots around psychoanalytic counselling, offer a path to social integration by way of the 'example' of an unproblematic racialised exemplar. If
an African-American family can achieve 'success' in Reagan's America (a
social dynamic intertextual with *The Cosby Show* (TV, 1984–92)), then why
not an 'outsider' like Martin Riggs? As Jeffords notes, this is also resonant
with the political and racial dynamics of the era during which Jesse Jackson
failed to achieve political power in that 'mainstream America was not prepared to perceive African-American men in the position of controlling and
defining justice' (1994: 138). She observes that it was important in this
respect that these renegade white males recognise the legitimacy of white
America, and reinforce rather than challenge it through their actions.

Injury, Repair and Restoration

The image of vulnerability that comes with graphic images of wounding or
injury would seem to suggest cracks in the facade of mythic invulnerability
woven around the hard body male. Yet these prove merely a bridge – a
consolidation of the position of resistance necessary before vengeance.
This is related to deeper issues around patrimony and power, and the relationship of the hero as the agent of action serving the broader interests of
society. Peter Hutchings remarks:

> Inasmuch as a man is the subject of patriarchy, then he has power.
> However this power is not his personal property, it does not emerge
> from within his own unique being. Rather it appertains to those
> institutional and ideological positions which the male individual
> occupies and through which he finds an identity. In this respect,
> power takes on an alienating quality: it can be used but it can
> never be owned. (1993: 92)

Hutchings is here speculating on the relationship between the male specta-
tor and scenes of evisceration, emasculation and destruction in the horror
genre, but the remark is applicable to the action film. Whereas the horror
film deals with bodily negation, the action film is concerned with restoration and repair. Again Jeffords becomes a useful frame of reference here
in her observation regarding the regenerative possibilities in the image
of masculinity. She remarks that 'the Reagan philosophy could ground

that social order not on increased authority or institutional power but on the enhanced power of the individual to determine his own future' (1994: 171). Thus Reaganite individualism, lionising the triumph of the hero in the name of an ideal of nation and identity based as much on rhetoric as policy, chimes neatly with the ability to effect self-repair and self-restoration, which acts of will in these films so obviously exemplify.

This is where the representation of wounding and wholesale violence differ in context. In *Bonnie and Clyde* (1967) and *The Wild Bunch*, both 'master genre' films (crime and western, respectively) the orgiastic violence represents absolute and utter destruction. In both cases the heroes' actions have led to this consequence – one set by defiance of the law, the other by moral choice. In either case the slow-motion explicit violence represents what Prince acknowledges to be 'a stylised rendition of violence' (2003: 175) giving greater intensity to the representation. Prince notes that the power of a slow-motion depiction of violent death is rooted in the sense of the body's loss of volition: in other words the erasure of its power of will as well as life. He notes that 'these slow-motion images derive their poetic force from the metaphysical paradox of the body's continued animate reactions during moments of diminished or extinguished consciousness' (2003: 184). He identifies that such scenes dramatise the moment of passing from conscious humanity to extinction of identity and personality, and sees the slow-motion death and the inanimate body twitches as a poetic intensification of that moment. The application of this technique across action films more broadly tends to be less aesthetically reflective, but the deployment of the device and its narrative effect remain – those who are filmed this way are those who are dead or dying.

The inflicting of a wound does not have the same effect, not in metaphysical terms anyway. The wound is a setback, a moment of pause, not an absolute constraint on further acts of volition. Self-repair scenes have been a feature of action films since the 1970s, markedly even in *Death Wish*, but very particularly in *First Blood*. In that film, Rambo leaps from a cliff to avoid a pursuing helicopter, a superheroic feat which marks a significant step from relative realism to hyperbolic spectacle. He falls through the branches of a tree, which, instead of breaking his limbs, tears a long gash in his right arm. The wound is significant, but not crippling – a description which also sums up the attitude towards his psychic wounds. If not quite the 'primal scene' of self-repair, it is a significant one. It demonstrates that the capacity for damage represented by the consequences of his action has resulted in a 'flesh wound' which necessitates pause. This can be healed though (the body can be mastered), permitting resumption of action and narrative momentum.

As Martin Frandley observes 'white male *ressentiment* is expressed cyclically through a masochistic aestheticisation of physical wounding and bodily punishment' (2004: 240). But its explicitness, its effect, must be represented, triggering an empathetic or arguably even kinesthetic response in the viewer. About three-quarters of the way through *Die Hard* a key scene occurs in which McClane attempts to pull large pieces of glass from his wounded feet. In obvious pain, he engages in conversation with Powell via walkie-talkie. McClane is trying to distract himself from his wounds, which the film makes clear by panning from Willis's face contorted mid-gag to his bloodied foot, out of which he extracts a particularly large shard of glass. The image is quite explicit, depicting blood and gore and evoking a sense of pain from the wound. It is not random violence, but up-close, personal bloody injury.

For McClane, the dialogue and the humour is masking the pain, but as the conversation turns serious the pain is transferred to the realm of emotional distress. McClane jokingly asks why Powell is not a street cop, asking if he has 'flat feet' (can the foot reference really be incidental?). Powell explains his personal trauma – shooting the child – which snaps McClane out of his forced whimsy and establishes a deeper empathetic bond between the men. The point is what meaning is ascribed to wound-

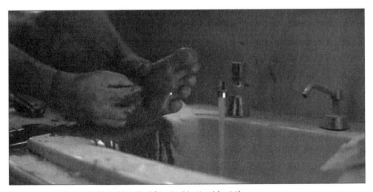

Human meat: Bruce Willis's bloodied foot in *Die Hard* (1988)

ing, and what value is placed on healing. The capacity to repair a physical wound indicates the potential to continue in a role of agency.

A similar set of conditions frames the self-repair sequences in *The Terminator*. The film on the whole is a virtual fugue of motion. It is a rhythmically specific contrapuntal alternation of scenes of movement arranged to create the sense of pursuit and to continually up the stakes of that pursuit. The Terminator itself (Arnold Schwarzenegger) is certainly relentless and shown to be constantly in motion: initially walking, later in vehicles, always with purpose – acquiring clothing, weapons, information and transport – with the single goal of killing Sarah Connor (Linda Hamilton), who, in the future, will give birth to the man who will win humanity's war against the machines. Its actions are inhibited by the intervention of Kyle Reese (Michael Beihn), a solider sent by Sarah's future son, John, to protect her.

It is after one such intervention that the Terminator must pause to effect self-repair, allowing it to disguise its inhumanity by carving away damaged tissue and removing a damaged eyeball. A puppet head is deployed to allow the representation of the sheared-away skin and the metal casing beneath it, and in particular to depict the empty eye socket behind which the Terminator's red mechanical 'eye' can be seen. The sequence concludes on a humourous note as the cyborg puts on a pair of dark sunglasses to cover its eye socket, then checks its hair in the mirror as if motivated by vanity. It then resumes its mission. In contrast, when Reese is wounded, it is Sarah who must tend to him, providing a moment of bonding for the couple, who will, as a consequence of this bond, experience the sexual encounter that will conceive John Connor. Again, in both cases, the emphasis on injury and repair is a narrative pause, another 'obstacle' to be overcome so that the will can be enacted, and, in the case of Reese and Sarah, through which a forward trajectory for all humanity is enabled.

The Terminator is quite specific in its overt speculation on the role of agency. Throughout the film, the narrative momentum matched by direction and editing of scenes of pursuit and combat, both on foot and in vehicles. It is a ritualised display of action and reaction, not unlike *Mad Max 2* in rhythmic economy. The Terminator acts; Reese reacts. They injure one another, pause, heal, then resume the fight. The Terminator, like the 'bricolage' vehicles in *Mad Max 2*, is gradually stripped of its literal and figurative excess baggage to the point where nothing is left but the metallic exoskeleton, which continues to pursue its target. Ultimately the film is about shaking Sarah out of her inert life and into a life of consequence (and agency) through the discovery of her strength. The Terminator is a catalyst. The trauma she experiences in being pursued is what awakens her power. At the climax of the film when Sarah and Reese are pursued by the exoskeletal Terminator, it is Sarah who urges an injured and exhausted Reese to his feet. She also gets to deliver a confrontational dispatch one-liner – 'you're terminated, fucker', she says – delivered with the teeth-gritted determination that would see fruition in Hamilton's characterisation of Sarah in *Terminator 2: Judgment Day*. By the end of the film, Sarah has learned to 'take action' and is represented in a state of motion. On the road, pregnant with John, and anticipating the disaster that is about to befall humanity, she is at last going somewhere.

The ultimate evocation of the healing capacities of the body through technological enhancement comes with *Robocop*. Here police officer Alex Murphy (Peter Weller) is murdered by a brutal gang before being 'resurrected' by a corporation eager to replace human police with robots. This is actually a fallback half-measure deployed only when the fully robotic ED-209 fails to perform to standard. The film is centered on the standard science fiction theme of the boundaries of humanity as defined by its technological development, but focused in terms of an image of injury, healing and repair.

The cyborg is sometimes spoken of in terms of a figure of postmodern liberation, most particularly in Donna Haraway's famous 'Cyborg Manifesto' where she notes that 'the cyborg is resolutely committed to partiality, irony, intimacy, and perversity. It is oppositional, utopian, and completely without innocence' (1991: 151). Steven Best is rather more skeptical of this particular cyborg however, noting that on the thematic level there are 'conflicting strains of conservative and progressive ideology' (1989: 26). What Best means by this is that though Murphy's resurrection as a cyborg would seem to represent an unsurpassable metaphor of injury and repair, it is arguable that the healing does not enable so much the exertion of will as indicate the limitations within which Murphy may act. He remains subject to the structures of technological capitalism that have 'healed' him.

The cyborg here is shown to be torn between the grip of two ideologies, one internal, one external. In internal terms, Murphy's restoration of his humanity signals the film's engagement with the politics of liberation and self-realisation. However, his path to realisation and redemption takes him through the external ideology of capitalist corporate villainy – an ideology that has been 'encoded' in his programming to prevent him arresting corporate executives. Recalling the Reaganite doctrine of self-realisation and its paradoxical relationship with empowerment, Murphy's 'liberation' in killing villainous Dick Jones (Ronny Cox) is actually nothing more than an internal corporate cleansing ('you're fired', yells the old man (Dan O'Herlihy), removing the prohibition on Murphy's actions). This leaves the corporate overlord free to continue to manipulate Murphy, which he duly does in *Robocop 2* (1990), where an even more lethal and uncontrollable cyborg incarnated from a drug lord wreaks havoc until it is put down by Murphy after an even more complex set of corporate directives are purged, restoring his primary programme to protect and serve.

If the action film represents recovery, renewal and hope as a rally against death, it is ironic that *Terminator 2: Judgment Day* should invoke both a sense of hope and of erasure. As in the first film, the struggle is for the survival of future humanity. However, there are several reversals, not least of all in the Terminator's new mission to protect the teenage John Connor (Edward Furlong), but also in Sarah's reasoning that the ultimate act of salvation would be to erase the future. To this end she encourages a guerilla campaign to destroy Cyberdine Systems, the company that will build the machines that declare war on humanity. By the end of the film the only remaining piece of that technology is the Terminator himself, who therefore must, and does, offer his own extinction as the ultimate redemption.

Jeffords addresses the film under the heading of 'terminal masculinity' (1994: 140), which she points out coincides with the Bush years rather than those of Reagan. In his inaugural address, President George H. W. Bush remarked that 'America is never wholly herself unless she is engaged in high moral principle. We as a people have such a purpose today. It is to make kinder the face of the Nation and gentler the face of the world' (1989). It is certainly in the light of this sentiment in the broadest and most rhetorical sense that the 'kinder, gentler Terminator' (a phrase used in more than one review of the film) emerges in *Terminator 2*, advertised with the catchline 'Same make. Same model. New mission.'

More significantly, the technological developments that allowed this film's villainous Terminator, the T-1000 (Robert Patrick), to shape-shift indicated a whole new paradigm for injury and repair. Composed of a liquid metal that allows it to shape-shift in cinematically engaging ways, the T-1000 displays the body as transitory and irrelevant. During the first confrontation between the 'classic' Terminator and the T-1000 in a shopping mall, shotgun wounds inflicted by the classic model are shown as mercury-like pools of shimmering silver that ripple over and then 'heal', restoring the body to an uninjured state. Throughout the film this becomes the means by which the stakes of action are intensified – the T-1000 cannot be injured and therefore, we presume, cannot be stopped. This reinforces the sense that the classic Terminator's mission is one of protection and defense rather than triumphal extinction of the enemy. The film's less hard-edged representation of the action hero (which is what the first film's villain now becomes), a hero who now, significantly, inflicts treatable wounds and healable injuries on human targets instead of dealing death, also coincides with the beginning of the political career of Schwarzenegger himself, under the demesne of the Bush Administration.

Gary Indiana has written scathingly of what he terms 'Schwarzenegger Syndrome', charting the slippage between the icon-image and persona of the star and his real career in American politics. Indiana observes that 'the total experience of having a relationship with Arnold Schwarzenegger that many people believed they had, and its transference from the world of make-believe into the arena of government, spoke to the possibility that the democratic experiment was rapidly mutating into a ceremonial fantasy' (2005: 60). One thought that this remark provokes is of the degree to which there is necessarily a separation between democratic government and fantasy, especially in the light of Jeffords' notion of the importance of rhetoric and culture in sustaining political ideology. It is certainly suggestive of such a correlation that Schwarzenegger's rise to global box-office dominance occurred during the Reagan era, and that his first association with political activity centred on Bush's Council on Physical Fitness and Sports. It is also significant, in this sense that an act of assisted suicide ('I cannot self-terminate'), together with a transparent focus on family and fatherhood (the Terminator becomes a surrogate father to John Connor, remarked upon by Sarah herself in the course of the film and examined by Jeffords and Tasker in this context), raises provocative associations between the concept of patrimony and agency in the action film. It also reflects a sense of the movement of the genre towards the self-erasing postmodernism that would ultimately destroy it, or, perhaps in the light of its return in a retrospective mode of which *Terminator Salvation* (2009) was part, wound it.

3   THE END OF IDEOLOGY

Irony and Excess

In *Rambo III* Rambo is compelled to leave a life of isolation in Tibet and journey to Afghanistan, where Colonel Trautman is being held by Soviet Intelligence. When preparing for his journey, loading up his equipment in more or less the classic 'suiting up' mode, a confederate wonders at a piece of his equipment – an ultraviolet light. The man asks Rambo what the object is. 'Blue light' says Rambo. 'What does it do?' asks the man, awestruck. 'Turns blue' Rambo responds, then resumes packing. John Rambo was not a character noted for his sense of humour in either of the previous films, but the pacing of this scene is clearly comic. There is, in fact, a continual presence of ironic humour throughout the film. When faced with the massed forces of the Soviet Army with only himself and Trautman seemingly available, Rambo comments: 'Well, surrounding them is out.' The ironies around the film became more pronounced when not long after its release, Soviet forces withdrew from Afghanistan, ending an occupation that had been in effect since 1979. The transparently propagandistic bent of the film, together with its assertion of the congruence between the political and the personal will in Rambo's struggle to galvanise native Afghani fighters in their battle against the Soviets, led to many amused commentators across the popular media chuckling that Rambo had driven the Soviets out of Afghanistan. This time no one was complaining about 'live moral issues' – everyone was in on the joke. The action film had become a neutered subject for passive consumption.

The increasing evident excess in the action film through the 1990s is key to understanding the process of deconstruction that underlies it. The defusing of tension is a refusal of anxiety, and thus, in narrative terms, denies or at least inhibits true motivation. This is analogous with what Žižek idenfies as the 'post-ideological' turn, in which a denial of hegemony constitutes a kind of ideological regression: 'Cynical denunciation (at the level of rational knowledge) is counteracted by the call of "irrational" belief' (2010: 70). This is a type of delusion hypothesis familiar from Marxist analyses, yet what Žižek has identified is the psychic phantasms of hegemonies divided against themselves without real struggle – a kind of meta-revolution in which no change is really possible because none is seen to be necessary – the illusion of choice suffices. One of the ways this operates in the post-classical action movie is through comedy. Raymond Durgnat observes that 'Much humour is moralistic, in its concern with deflating or ridiculing angry, erotic, or other anti-social and authentic feelings. Further, much humour exists in order to kathart such feelings, that is, to diminish their intensity by a brief, non-commital, scarcely understood, indulgence' (1969: 40).

The films of Arnold Schwarzenegger most evinced this tendency. His flat, accented delivery of consciously comic one-liners became as anticipated as Hitchcock cameos and were essential in his association with the lighter side of the hard body. His career had actually begun primarily in comedy. He played to his own image as a bodybuilding icon in *Stay Hungry* (1976), where even Gary Indiana concedes that he 'displayed his ability to project a personality considerably more nuanced than, and even at times surprisingly unlike, the stereotype of slow-witted eminence in a submental marginal sport his body itself suggested' (2005: 34). Indiana also notes Schwarzenegger's uncanny ability to project a smiling self-confidence intertextual with the film roles with which the public still associates him. This was used with particular force at the Republican National Convention in 2004 in support of President George W. Bush. As J. Hoberman writes:

When the Arnold takes his super-guzzling, militarised Humvee on the road or holds court in his Bedouin-style smoking tent, when he compares the legislature to a kindergarten, when he calls state senators 'girlie men' and threatens to terminate them, when he boasts of dominating the state's nurses, he is inviting us to relive his greatest hits. (2005: 34)

He also notes that 'It allows for embracing, in so-called real life, the Neanderthal homilies and bully-boy will-to-power that the Arnold's movies have always concealed behind the fig leaf of self-reflexive irony' (ibid.).

This 'fig leaf' is important in understanding the role of self-deflating humour in the action film. In spite of appearances, humour does not undercut the basic narrative, thematic or ideological thrust. Instead, it allows audiences to treat what they see with what Durgnat calls 'scarcely understood indulgence' (1969: 40). In this way the film *Commando* (1985), for example, becomes a nexus of homophobic and homoerotic elements, centred on the slightly pudgy, mustachioed and clearly gay villain Bennett (Vernon Wells – who also played the crazed, mohawked homosexual raider Wez in *Mad Max 2*).

Bennett's deviance is contrasted with Matrix's (Schwarzenegger) patrimonial heterosexuality (the film revolves around Matrix's attempt to rescue his kidnapped daughter (Alyssa Milano)). And yet, at the climax of the film when Bennett and Matrix face off in a steam-filled sub-basement surrounded by sweaty pipes, Matrix bare-chested and wounded, there is a moment of clear homoerotic charge. Matrix is clutching his wounded, bleeding arm, his perfect muscles bathed in sweat. He is attempting to persuade Bennett to put away his gun and let the girl go. In a seductive invitation, lowering his voice into a soft, pleading tone, Matrix says 'put a knife in me, look me in the eye and see what's going on in there when you turn it' (do we even need Freud here?). As Matrix moves slowly towards Bennett, his own knife drawn, a series of cutaways reveals Bennett becoming visibly excited.

A brutal combat scene ensues in which Schwarzenegger's bare upper body receives numerous heavy blows from Wells, who wears a sleeveless top overlaid with chain mail. It seems as though Bennett is going to win. 'How does it feel to be a dying man, John?' he asks, invoking the ultimate trauma. The response is characteristic – Matrix spits 'bullshit' and unleashes a series of powerful hooks and uppercuts rapidly and discontinuously edited to create the impression of greater speed and intensity. Bennett falls back, then, realising he has been bested in physical contest, draws an Uzi from his belt and says 'I'm not going to shoot you between the eyes, John, I'm going to shoot you between the balls.' Matrix rips a steam pipe from the wall and hurls it at Bennett, impaling him. Blood gushes from Bennett's mouth where he stands, the pipe having penetrated his body and gone through to a boiler behind him. Steam is emerging from the pipe in a doubling of this plainly ejaculatory set of emissions (blood, steam). Matrix, unperturbed, quips 'Let off some steam, Bennett.'

Indiana remarks that Schwarzenegger's 'gay friendly' image dates to the post-Stonewall culture of mainstream homosexual fetishism of muscled bodies like Schwarzenegger's. In the documentary *Pumping Iron* (1977) it is clear in the scene where he performs in a prison (inmates whistle and hoot and he smiles broadly and jokes 'I've heard about you guys' while wagging a playful finger) that he is aware of his homosexual appeal. If this scene in *Commando* is not testament to his willingness to trade on this image while also erasing any genuine doubt about his ultimate heterosexual masculinity, then nothing is. As Indiana remarks: 'The consistent assertion of his basic heterosexual identity makes the "gay friendly" identification easily reversible, in rhetorically well-crafted increments, should it develop into a liability in the years ahead' (2005: 27).

Ironic humour has been deployed throughout the action film in similarly ambiguous ways across several contexts. We have already seen an example of this in *48 Hrs.* where racial bigotry is defused by the application of the buddy principle – diminishing the intensity, as Durgnat might say. The same process is at work across many Eddie Murphy films, including *Beverly Hills Cop* where Axel Foley's narrative and linguistic confrontation of white privilege is by no means an assertion of radical politics. A similarly self-conscious racial collision is depicted in *Passenger 57* (1992). In this *Die Hard* on a plane, race supplants if not completely replaces class as the subtextual context. Air Marshall John Cutter (Wesley Snipes) faces sociopath Charles Rane (Bruce Payne), a prisoner in transport who has hijacked a passenger jet upon which Cutter is travelling. In a key 'taunting on the telephone' scene where Rane is threatening Cutter, Cutter asks 'ever play roulette?' Rane responds sardonically, 'On occasion.' Cutter, his face and hand contrasting with the light-coloured telephone and surrounding airline interior, snaps: 'Always bet on black.'

Racial badinage is also a key feature of *Bad Boys* (1995) where police detectives Mike Lowrey (Will Smith) and Marcus Burnett (Martin Lawrence) perform a bickering buddy act in the midst of a variety of racially inflammatory conflicts. The difference here is that both men are black, so they, like Axel Foley, represent an undivided opposition to the white (criminal) orthodoxies that surround them. Perhaps the apotheosis comes in *Bad Boys II* (2003) where the pair disrupt a Ku Klux Klan meeting posing as Klan members (can anyone take this scene seriously if they have seen *Blazing Saddles* (1974)?). After dramatically discarding their robes and pulling their weapons on the assembled Klan members, the veneer of intimidation breaks down when Burnett fluffs the lyrics to their theme song. The setting and subject are clearly fraught with meaning from a social and racial point of view, but the rhetorical force is negated entirely by transparent irony.

The same could be said of the hyperstimulated representation of 'women warriors' throughout the era, beginning with comparatively legiti-mate matriarchal conflict between Ripley (Sigourney Weaver) and the Alien Queen in *Aliens* (1986) (exaggerated, to be sure, but paradigmatically effective), through the critically lauded rogue cop film *Blue Steel* (1989) in which, as Kevin Ferguson (2008) observes, the feminist heroine takes on the iconic masculine figure of the yuppie devil. This continued through the traumatised hardbody Sarah Connor of *Terminator 2: Judgment Day*, which, as Jeffords notes, effectively derogates her maternal role to the Terminator itself, the reformed junkie of *Nikita* (1990) (remade as *The Assassin* (1993)) with its *Pygmalion* overtones, and the female time-bomb/cyborg of *Eve of Destruction* (1991). The trope then evolved through ever-greater levels of exaggeration and ultimately self-implosive post-classicism with the likes of *Barb Wire* (1996) in which Pamela Anderson played the comic-strip heroine of the title, *The Long Kiss Goodnight* (1996) in which Geena Davis played an amnesiac assassin whose discovery of her capacity to act is in contrast with the role of traditional femininity she has assumed following the accident which caused her to lose her memory, and *G.I. Jane* (1997), a war movie consciously placing images of masculinity and feminity in con-flict in the setting of body conditioning as a woman (Demi Moore) trains to become a Navy SEAL. The conscious 'insertion' of a hardbody heroine sat as uncomfortably with feminists as it seemed often to deny a unique femaleness of expression in favour of a straight co-opting of the masculine role. Filmmakers, for their part, seemed uncertain what to do with them until they simply stopped trying to take them seriously.

Terminator 3: Rise of the Machines (2003) attempts to use a female Terminator (Kristanna Loken) to capture the lean intensity of Robert

Patrick's T-1000, but undercuts itself through self-conscious hyperfemini-sation. Instead of commanding her targets to give her their clothes or cars as direct commands of action like her 'male' predecessor, this Terminator expresses her desire for things in terms of lifestyle choice: 'I like your car', she says. Meanwhile, Schwarzenegger's arrival as the 'good' Terminator is absolutely tongue-in-cheek and gender conscious. His search for apparel takes him to a hick bar where it is ladies' night, and his nudity is taken as part of the show. He acquires clothing from an effete male stripper, and departs to hoots and hollers of appreciation from the unharmed assembly. As a final gag, he slips on a pair of star-shaped and spangled sunglasses retrieved from the stripper's jacket.

The deconstructive apex of the female action hero came with *Charlie's Angels* (2000) and its sequel *Charlie's Angels: Full Throttle* (2003), a hyperstylised, hyperfetishised, hysterical postmodernist pastiche based on the popular television series (US 1976–81) that was, even in its own time, perceived not so much to represent feminist liberation (which is its theme – three female police officers resisting sexism in the workplace become private detectives) but a mainstream blacklash and streaming of feminist energy into consumerism. Anna Gough-Yates uses the title of a popular early episode – 'Angels in Chains' – as the title of her essay on the series (2001: 83). She acknowledges that in spite of the constraint placed upon progressive feminism by this representation, the theme represents a level of engagement – not dissimilar to the apologia for comic racism. This applies entirely to the 2000 film, which though 'playful' to be sure,

Posthuman feminism? Drew Barrymore, Cameron Diaz and Lucy Liu kick against the pricks in *Charlie's Angels* (2000)

completely subscribes to every cultural cliché around the representation of women that exists. The opening scene of *Charlie's Angels: Full Throttle* may critique the hooting, hollering men who stand and watch Natalie (Cameron Diaz) bump and grind on a mechanical bull wearing thigh highs and a cowboy hat, because they are all being duped for the purpose of mission, but they're still hooting and hollering, as are the audience if the invitation presented by the gaze of the camera upon Diaz's moving body is anything to go by.

Gough-Yates's critique of *Charlie's Angels* can be extended to encompass the entire endeavour of the hardbody heroine. In terms remarkably similar to Robinson (1998) Gough-Yates concludes that these texts 'offer women viewers an entertaining – and satisfying – avenue through which they can make sense of their social and cultural lives. The effectiveness of these responses as a political strategy is obviously limited – and possibly detracts from feminism as a collective form of social action' (2001: 97). The same applies to the hyper-feminisation of Angelina Jolie in the adventure film *Lara Croft: Tomb Raider* (2001) – a woman free of economic constraint who pursues adventure for stimulation, not from necessity. Though Marc O'Day would glowingly comment that this and other such films are 'luminous examples of the cinema's ability to create beauty in motion' (2004: 216) this sounds rather like a restatement of a very old set of spectatorial conventions.

Much the same can be said of subsequent Jolie vehicles *Mr. and Mrs. Smith* (2005), *Wanted* (2008) and *Salt* (2010), although the latter, ironically, was originally written for a male lead. A brief attempt to deepen the complexity of the 'action babe' seemed to come with *Hanna* (2011), where a pre-adolescent assassin goes rogue. Elements of Angela Carteresque adult fairy tale mystique are woven through the hard-edged action scenes, and the film evinces none of the troubling paedophilic undercurrents noted in both *Léon* (1994) and *Kick-Ass* (2010). However normal hard/sexy body service was resumed quickly in both *Colombiana* (2011) and *Haywire* (2011), the latter of which could at least boast of an actual female athelete (Gina Carano) in the lead.

Given that homophobia, racism and sexism persist in society, one would have to disagree that irony proves another weapon in the arsenal of a cinema of action insofar as such a cinema represents a form of mediated reaction. On the contrary, in incorporating ironic self-reflection the social provocation at the centre of the genre is negated. It is hard to conceive now of the kind of outcry that surrounded *Death Wish* or *Rambo: First Blood Part II* being generated by an action film. Throughout the late 1990s in films like *The Rock* (1996), *Con-Air* (1996) and *Executive Decision* (1996), tropes and formulae enabled occasional reference to philosophical precepts or social traumas (Gulf War syndrome, prison reform, terrorism), but rarely generated a sense of political anxiety. As Prince (2009) argues, the characterisation of sympatheic antagonists as disaffected social rebels tends to shift into a mode of denial more characteristic of what Žižek is talking about by making them mentally unbalanced, fundamentally criminal or irrationally angry. Prince notes the moral confusion in these films, comparing the clear political motivations of real-life terrorists with their fictive counterparts, and noting that the fantasy of an organised (action-heroic, reactive) response is in contrast to the prevailing confusions of counterterrorism in Clinton and Bush Jr America. It is this that presents us with the most powerful deconstructive energy within the genre in this period – its double idenfication with the antisocial action hero and the antisocial nemesis in light of the meta-text created by self-awareness. The post-classical mode thereby disengages the audience's expectation that their involvement should be at the level of discourse, critique or articulation of ideology – there is no ideology, really, right?

Death by Deconstruction

By the early 1990s, action films existed in a world where action films existed, and were, increasingly, associated with the fading ideologies of the Cold War. In *Demolition Man* (1993) there was an ironic articulated self-awareness in the fact that its central characters, a rogue cop played by Sylvester Stallone and a flamboyantly anti-social villain played by Wesley Snipes, were both cryogenically frozen and resuscitated in a peaceful future where they are out of step with a society and culture now dominated by peaceful post-ideological consensus and political correctness. In a key scene early in the film, as uber-villain Simon Phoenix escapes from a hi-tech prison with relative ease, the futuristic, pacifist police department are able only to watch their monitors in dumbfoundment; incapable of action and confused by the criminal violation '187 – Murder/Death/Kill' which the computer tells them has been committed. The genre could not sustain its classicism amid the new epistemological uncertainties of Clinton-era post-modern America, so instead entered a phase of what Peter Krämer would describe in terms of post-classical Hollywood on the whole as a phase of 'defamiliarisation and assimilation' (1998: 307).

Krämer notes that a shift from classical to post-classical cinema does not represent a complete break with tradition. He, like Tag Gallagher (2003) argues that many features of a 'new' or post-classical cinema have long-reaching historical precedent. This reminds us of Steven Neale's (2003) assertion that it is the *predominance* of elements that defines the characterisation of a genre, not merely their presence. The question is then: what are the predominant features of the action film in this period and how do they problematise the concept of agency?

Thomas Elsaesser and Warren Buckland (2002) give an example of classical and post-classical reading using *Die Hard* as their case study. From a classical point of view, they argue, *Die Hard* represents an ideologically-loaded character-driven disruption-and-resolution formula. However, they argue that in post-classical terms, by which they suggest lie 'more along the lines of an excessive classicism, rather than as a rejection or absence of classicism' (2002: 61), the film is textually reflexive of the conditions of its own production. As a 'high concept' blockbuster, they observe, 'how often the film puts on show its own rhetoric, as well as the ideological material it is supposed to transport and transform' (2002: 64). They argue that the film is a reflective, allusive, more self-consciously unstable narrative than a classical model would support. It is, after all, a film about the defence of a blatantly phallic corporate edifice by a character versed in heroic cinema – 'another orphan of a bankrupt culture who thinks he's John Wayne, Rambo, Marshall Dillon?' as uber-villain Hans Gruber (Alan Rickman) puts it. The reference to Rambo is so contemporary that it demands recognition of the audience's collusion with this experience of narratology.

Elsaesser and Buckland remark that one of the primary markers of a post-classical film is that 'from the perspective of production, post-classical films stand in a tradition: they have mastered the code of the classical, and they are not afraid to display this mastery as "play"' (2002: 79); in other words certain films demonstrate an awareness of their own construction and placement within discourses of culture, society and cinematic aesthetics. By the early to mid-1990s 'play' with the formula to the point of self-parody was evident in films like *Road House* (1989) and *Point*

Break (1991) with its hysterical masculine archetypes and barely concealed homoeroticism exemplifying what David Greven identifies as a split masculinity where 'masculinity became aware of itself both as monolith *and* joke' (2009: 16), creating a meta-textual space in which the very status of masculinity and its associations with agency where subject to conscious address. In films like *The Running Man* (1987), *Tango & Cash* (1989), *The Last Boy Scout* (1991), *Under Siege* (1992) and *Speed*, the genre was now so transparently formulaic and self-aware of 'play' with convention, that it barely needed the counterpoint of parodies like *The Hard Way* (1991), *Hot Shots! Part Deux* (1993) and *National Lampoon's Loaded Weapon 1* (1993) (or, much later, *Hot Fuzz* (2007)) to render its tenets as farce. Action movies had become so allusive to their own short histories that it was only a matter of time before the genre collapsed in on itself, as represented by the very conscious enacting of such an epistemological crisis in *Last Action Hero*.

This film takes the negation of classicism as its subject. Jonathan Romney says the quality of self-parody in action movies is a conscious signal of distance from themselves, a marker of 'tongue-in-cheek' that marks *Lethal Weapon 2* and *Die Hard 2* (1990) from their predecessors. He notes: 'These films try to pass themselves off as being at least more honest about their own automatism. But *Last Action Hero* goes one step further. It is neither more dishonest nor more honest than those "real" action thrillers; it simply takes self-awareness to an extreme' (1993: 7). Eric Lichtenfeld calls it 'the apotheosis of self-parody for both the genre and for Hollywood as a whole' (2007: 342). The film follows schoolboy Danny Madigan (Austin O'Brien), an action film fanatic, on a journey literally through the screen. He is given a magic ticket that transports him from the dark reality of contemporary New York to the brightly-lit fantasy of 'movie' Los Angeles. There he encounters his hero 'Jack Slater' (Arnold Schwarzenegger) in the midst of his latest film. The catch is that Danny knows Jack Slater is a character played by Arnold Schwarzenegger, and knows action movies are not real. However, the magic ticket has brought him into a universe where they are real, and he is in real danger. When the villainous Mr Benedict (Charles Dance) uses the ticket to enter the 'real' world where evil can triumph, Danny and Slater must pursue him there.

At the climax of the film, a premiere of the film-within-the-film, 'Jack Slater IV', Slater meets Arnold Schwarzenegger. In a scene of almost unbearable directness, Schwarzenegger portrays himself as a shallow, commercially-minded media-hog (Maria Shriver, playing herself, warns 'don't plug the restaurant, I hate it when you plug the restaurant' in reference to the Planet Hollywood chain, then co-owned by Schwarzenegger, Stallone and Bruce Willis). When he meets Slater, he assumes he is a studio-hired celebrity impersonator, and begins cajoling him to do shopping centre openings on his behalf, at which point Slater rounds on him and says, 'Look, I don't really like you, you've brought me nothing but pain', signalling a rather startling ironic distance between the 'real' Schwarzenegger persona (which is not sympathetic) and the idealised hardbody hero he is playing.

The film's resolution hinges on a doubling of its opening scene (from 'Jack Slater III') in which Slater's son dies during a shoot-out with the Ripper (Tom Noonan). Brought into the 'real world' by Benedict, the Ripper restages the moment with Danny in place of Slater's son. From Slater's point of view as a fictional character this is a classic traumatic scene, and his rescue of Danny a classic moment of redemption. It is then that the film segues to its 'real world' climax as Benedict shoots Jack in the chest. Before he can deliver the *coup de grace*, Danny manages to knock him over and Slater is able to defeat him ('no sequel for you' he says). But, in the action film's most absurdly explicit evocation of death anxiety, the magic ticket floats into an art-house cinema where *The Seventh Seal* (1957) is playing. This prompts the figure of Death (played in the Bergman film by Bengt Ekerot, but here impersonated by Ian McKellen) to enter the 'real' world. As Danny attempts to get Jack back into the movie world, where his injury is 'just a flesh wound', Death advances.

There is an extraordinary rhetorical and epistemological oscillation in this scene. McKellen is clearly not Ekerot so the real/fake mirror upon which the film has relied is erased. Worse, it seems he really is a personification of death, demonstrated when he touches a man in the 'real' world on the shoulder who collapses and dies. When Death approaches Jack, Danny draws Benedict's enormous .357 Dan Wesson revolver on him and makes a speech to the effect that he has 'had enough' of him. Danny's despair may be understandable in the context of the surprisingly bleak portrait of the 'real world' that the film paints. Director John McTiernan casts New York as an almost nightmarish place. When Danny attempts to sneak out to see the Slater film, he is instantly mugged by a knife-wielding thug. When Benedict callously shoots a mechanic to see if anyone will care (which they

Resisting mortality: Austin O'Brien defends Arnold Schwarzenegger from Death in *Last Action Hero* (1993)

don't), the scene is more chilling than funny given the absolute silence of an oblivious city. The suggestion in this scene is perhaps that Danny cannot face reality. Being the surrogate for the audience, that is perhaps too direct a message. Even worse though, Death reveals that he was 'only curious' about Jack because he does not appear on any of his lists – ie he is not going to die – then says: 'Though *you* are, Daniel.' Though Death assures him this happens when he is a 'grandfather', the moment is shocking in the context of a comic action thriller with a child protagonist – this child will die, as will we all. No sequel for you, then.

In many respects, *Last Action Hero* is an effective evisceration of the conventions of the action film and also a reasonable rendition of the same formula. Its narrative duology allows the space for irony the audience had come to expect, and the action scenes in the film are staged with the skill and scale you might expect from McTiernan. However, it was a critical disaster and a financial failure. The film failed to recover even its estimated production budget of $120m (marketing costs not included) between both domestic and overseas box office.

James Robert Parish (2006) gives a detailed account of the making of the film, which involved significant behind-the-scenes wrangling just to get to the working screenplay. At stake in the production of this film was the ever-spiralling cost of blockbuster entertainments, especially in the wake of *Terminator 2: Judgment Day*, which had grossed some $500m. Parish recounts how *Last Action Hero* seemed set to become an industry whipping boy before it reached test screenings. In this respect it is not even the fact of the film's directness of address that proved at the root of its pariah status – the film is emblematic of the 'high concept' production methodologies that had become so dominant.

As Jerry Bruckheimer and Don Simpson became the foremost names in action movie line management, the enterprise and dealmaking capacity to 'sell the package' became as important as the content of the package. In contrast to the rigidly direct ideology underlying the ascension of the action film, it became a looser post-classical construction within which the audience expectation and anticipation upon which a genre is at least partly built became an element of its self-destruction. In a constant attempt to second guess the audience and out-spectacle each new spectacle, the action film became at once distended and inert. It was no longer a register of momentum, but increasingly, a sign of blind panic in the film industry about itself, desperate to find larger and larger canvases upon which to paint spectacles that would draw audiences to them.

The post-classical aesthetic also involves the much-observed acceleration of editing patterns and increased 'spectacularism', exemplified by the films of Michael Bay, including *The Rock* and *Bad Boys*. As Lichtenfeld observes, Bay's experience as a commercial music video director, working in compressed timeframes of two or three minutes, produced a sense of visual energy that is almost definitively excessive. Film aesthetics in this era go well beyond Bordwell's 'expressive amplification' and into 'intensified continuity' (Bordwell 2002: 232, 16) where, as he points out, feature films appear more like trailers for themselves. Bordwell also points out though that the basic styles of shooting and editing in an 'intensified' mode have been in use since the beginnings of cinema, seen in the work of Sergei Eisenstein and Abel Gance. He also makes the claim that this intensified cinema is not even post-classical, but merely a refinement of classical style.

A vital contribution to this argument is made in the edited volume by Wanda Strauven (2006), where the representational paradigms of the contemporary 'spectacular' cinema are compared with scholarly framing of the origins of the cinema itself as a 'cinema of attractions'. The proposition is made that the most important feature of both the classic and the contemporary cinema of spectacle is the measure of direct address to the audience. Just as early audiences were confronted by a shocking modernist way of seeing, so it can be argued that the postmodern configuration represents an ongoing process of conceiving of postmodern (and arguably even post-human) society. However, as Dick Tomasovic points out, the industrial model defining the millennial cinema represents a very different set of defining parameters. He notes Hollywood 'constitutes itself, blockbuster after blockbuster, in an aesthetics differentiated from the early cinema of attractions: its current mode of functioning is an overstatement with which it sentences itself to a logic of self-consuming and incessant hybridisation, to a perpetual crisis of aesthetics' (2006: 318).

The most significant feature of this post-classical aesthetic in terms of this book though is that this intensified, heightened, hysterical cinema could not be contained by the action film as a genre. The world of the action film is quite bound – restricted by the limits of the physical and social body as agent, which as we have seen is in a state of compulsion, restriction and restraint from which it attempts to escape and destroy that which constraints it. As the body became more unbound even the hyperbolic muscleman was not enough to handle things. The superhero genre experienced a rebirth at this time, with the release of *Batman* (1989) beginning of a string of spectacular economic successes. Lichtenfeld discusses the superhero film, but in terms of the current analysis, the genre represents too great a shift in framework for full consideration. Suffice to note that once you move to the realms of 'a man dressed up as a bat' as the Joker (Jack Nicholson) says in *Batman*, you have moved into a different argument. It is this as much as anything that may account for the failure of *Judge Dredd* (1995) in which the satiric caricature of a future fascist society fell afoul of incongruous cinematic registers, leaving Stallone unable to navigate a space between postmodern irony and hardbody heroism in his portrayal of the (literally) iconic comic book character. The more downbeat (and lower budget) 2012 iteration, entitled *Dredd 3D*, fared slightly better in avoiding such irony. Even the most 'realistic' of comic book heroes, Marvel's 'The Punisher' (inspired by 1970s vigilantes) proved unable to gain traction in either the 1980s *The Punisher* (1989) or twice in the 2000s *The Punisher* (2004) and *Punisher: War Zone* (2008).

As the industry craved bigger and better spectacles, the geographical canvas also became broader. The setting was outer space like in *Star Wars Episode I: The Phantom Menace* (1999), monster-infested jungles as in *The Lost World: Jurassic Park* (1997) or purely fantastical realms as in *The Lord of the Rings: The Fellowship of the Ring* (2001). At this point, we are no longer in the realms of the action film, but in science fiction, adventure and fantasy. Likewise as the levels of spectacular destruction grew even greater the frames of reference moved from death anxiety to extinction anxiety. This led to the return of the disaster movie, offering an entirely different set of pleasures for the audience. As Kim Newman observes: 'The more complicated a civilisation becomes, the more fun it is to imagine the whole works going up in flames' (2000: 18). In films including *Independence Day*, *Twister* (1996), *Dante's Peak* (1997), *Volcano* (1997) and *Armageddon* the intensified visual style of the post-classical action film was deployed to represent ever-mounting incidents of destruction. Though arguably the ultimate cinema of reaction in that sense, the disaster film again constitutes another significant shift in analytical framework; one explored in volumes by Newman, Stephen Keane (2006) and John Sanders (2009).

Lichtenfeld does make particular mention of *Armageddon* as a key moment in that it was around this film that the most intense criticism of contemporary spectacularism revolved, and the most direct attacks upon the filmmaking of director Michael Bay. He cites Todd McCarthy of *Variety*, who wrote that the film 'decisively crosses the line from mindless, relatively painless garbage into a whole new dimension of summer-movie hell. Like being yelled at by idiots for 144 minutes, the *Armageddon* experience is pointlessly traumatising' (see Lichtenfeld 2007: 220). This summative observation, and particularly McCarthy's use of the word 'trauma', raises a rather fascinating question – to what extent might the experience of postmodernism itself become the centre of a strain of neo-classical action movie? We will explore this in the final chapter.

'I Know Kung-Fu': The Body Unbound

In *The Matrix* prophet/rebel leader Morpheus (Laurence Fishburne) wishes to test the abilities of Neo (Keanu Reeves), who may be the digital messiah foretold to liberate the enslaved human race from an illusory computer simulation. Morpheus brings Neo to a training ground called 'the construct'. Here the conditions of the simulated reality are controlled human operators. Morpheus chooses to test Neo's strength through combat. When they begin, he has no skills, but when Morpheus instructs his operators to upload the training programme Neo experiences a sudden rush marking his instantaneous acquisition of an extensive knowledge of martial arts. His eyes flicker, then snap open and he exclaims: 'I know kung-fu!'

Such a learning process would come as cold comfort to Hong Kong martial artists. One of the standard scenes in a Hong Kong martial arts film is the training montage. This reflects the harsh reality of a lifetime (and childhood) spent training under notoriously harsh conditions in Peking Opera. The pain and suffering of physical learning which primes the body to react and move in the elaborate ways required to carry out a bewildering array of stunts and movements in these films is absolutely necessary, and feeds into the experience of the art for those who practice it.

David Bordwell remarks that this quality of authenticity informs the division between the aesthetics of action cinema in Hong Kong and America. When a Hong Kong actor takes a blow, it is 'performed', but real enough to register genuine impact. When a Hollywood star is in a situation of jeopardy, insurance regulations and the desire to see the real actor for as much time as possible means that films must compensate stylistically for their inability to portray genuine danger. For Bordwell, this is the root of the problem of clarity and legibility characteristic of intensified continuity. He remarks: 'when fans praise a [John] Woo or Ring Lam sequence for its "continuous action", I'm suggesting a slight correction. It's Hollywood that relies on nonstop bustle, and the sequence often suffers from it' (2008: 406). In Hong Kong, by contrast, the capacity to capture precise actions filmed as they are carried out, and the necessity to understand the flow of such movements across a scene or sequence is characteristic of directors who are often also actors and trained fighters. This contributes to both the drama and the poetry of this depiction of action.

Exoticism was part of the success of the 'first wave' of Shaw Brothers and Bruce Lee films in the West. Rosalind Coward and John Ellis described 'a cinema of difference, exotic and vaguely indecipherable, full of gnomic encounters and violence that was ritualised according to fantasies of wish-fulfillment' (1981: 93). This is descriptive of what the Western action film would evolve into, but had not yet when Hong Kong films first began to appear abroad. Bruce Lee's early death would leave the majority of his film work framed by cultish exoticism, but his physical artistry remains undeni-able. As Anderson (1998) noted, Lee's on-screen movement feeds into the core of a kinesthetic experience of action film by prompting a desire to emulate his precision, grace, speed and power. The bravura 'cavern battle' sequence in *Enter the Dragon* remains a stunning display of fluency of form both unarmed and with a range of weapons. However, this film, which was an international co-production, aside, Lee's films would mainly reside within the broader Hong Kong and Chinese tradition. That said, as Coward and Ellis point out, there are signs of an appropriation of elements of the American style, notably Peckinpah.

Lee's films do nonetheless mainly fall within a classic martial arts demesne, and Coward and Ellis further delineate the cultural and spiritual values represented across these and other films. They note that Confucian teachings of patriarchal duty and loyalty underlie many of the revenge-based plots. Buddhist conceptions of perfection and attainment of age and wisdom feed into the 'mentor' characters that are a frequent feature. Taoist philosophy's sense of the value of nature and the evil of the artificial together with an emphasis on frugality clearly feeds a great deal of the emphasis on the body itself as a weapon when honed, refined and trained. The authors remark that when presented as thematic abstractions (as opposed to philosophical arguments within particular disciplines) 'these notions have a deceptive air of familiarity. The real difficulty for us faced with the swordplay film was the unexpected combination and modulation of these notions. The narratives often seem to offer a trite problematic, yet it develops in unexpected ways' (1981: 94).

Stephen Teo (1997), Hector Rodriguez (1997) and Tony Williams (2000) further explore the national context of this cinema (Valentina Vitali (2010) has done likewise for Hindi action cinema), which at least partly resolves this dilemma of reception. Teo points out that from a Chinese perspective, Bruce Lee's films are politically nationalistic, espousing strength, duty and honour to proffer an image of Chinese masculinity that was capable, powerful and unifying (1997: 110–21). This is actually the subject of *Jing Wu Men* (*Fist of Fury*, 1972) in which a Chinese martial arts student defies both Japanese racist imperialism and Buddhist pacifism. Against the wishes of his peers, Zhen takes action and rebels against the repressive Japanese authorities, for which he is eventually killed. Rodriguez and Williams respectively focus on films based on real-life martial artist and anti-imperial political activist Huang Feihong which, as Rodriguez says of the earlier varieties, operate 'by combining a heightened realism with a renewed respect for national traditions, but also to disseminate messages that would enhance the moral stature of cinema audiences along Confucian lines' (1997: 15). This would continue right through to the Tsui Hark/Huang Feihong films, beginning with *Once Upon a Time in China*

(1991), which proved a star-making turn for Jet Li (who would go on to feature in the remake of *Fist of Fury*, *Jing Wu Ying Xiong* (*Fist of Legend* (1994)). Though the context of Confucianism would certainly not carry to the US, the overall project of remasculination and national identity is, as we have seen, quite parallel.

In question here, though, is the appropriation of elements of the martial arts film across the Western action movie, particularly in the post-classical period. This was arguably partly consciously in reaction to the increasing staleness of the hyperbolic style and the desire to inject an element of the unfamiliar into the routine. It actually begins much earlier, with the rise of Chuck Norris. Norris's legitimate status as six times world middleweight Karate champion was much touted throughout the 1970s, and his featuring in films was seen as a means to bring the exotic appeal of martial arts to otherwise conventional and more aesthetically rigid American genre pieces. He made a notable debut in the Bruce Lee-directed *Meng long guo jiang* (*The Way of the Dragon*, 1972), where his bulky hirsute body was contrasted with Lee's smooth, lithe and agile form. Here Lee was deploying Norris's Western exoticism as an Occidentalist 'other' – the nemesis that must be overcome. Ironically, it would be Norris who would then colonise the Asian mode of expression that was martial arts itself, reframing it for an Occidental audience.

Norris developed an identifiably rugged and Western persona through films featuring his capacity to deploy both martial arts and conventional weapons including the trucker film *Breaker! Breaker!* (1977), the rogue cop movie *An Eye for an Eye* (1981), and the 'new western' *Lone Wolf McQuade*, culminating in his long-running television series *Walker, Texas Ranger* (1992–2001). In many respects, *Lone Wolf McQuade* replays elements of *Coogan's Bluff* including a remarkably similar opening scene which involves McQuade outwitting Mexican arms dealers in the desert, and consistently representing a confrontation between the corruption of refined capitalism and the heroism of hardened frontier individualism. The interlinkage with notions of American identity rooted in the western genre could not be more obvious. What was important about Norris's cinema though was the sense that his physicality could not be bound by generic limits: that a new vocabulary of action needed to be deployed to see him 'in action' – kicking, leaping, punching with the force of a cowboy and the grace of a samurai.

It was this sense of the unbounding of the body, the exceeding of physical capacity that was at stake in the increased presence of Asian motifs and methodologies in American action films throughout the 1990s and beyond. In this Leon Hunt (2004) notes that *The Matrix* represents the most prominent convergence of this trend with the use of digital imaging technologies to compensate for the physical limitations of American actors. Hunt goes so far as to describe this as a transnational cinema, though it is the largely dramatic and reflective poetry of *Wu hu cang long* (*Crouching Tiger, Hidden Dragon*, 2000) that earns this particular, avowedly optimistic, recognition.

Nevertheless, from the mid-1990s there was an increasing Asian presence in the Western action movie. A stream of mainly direct-to-video releases of Hong Kong theatrical films established a solid fanbase, but, as Bordwell points out, mainly within adolescent subculture (2000: 90). Ironically, possibly the most visible success from these was American-born Cynthia Rothrock, who, as Tasker points out, brought with her a key aspect of the Hong Kong action film – the prevalence of women as figures of strength and action without a lingering sense of novelty. Naturalised through strategies of ironic humour and geographical containment (localisation – she is a town sheriff in *China O'Brien* (1990)). Tasker maintains that 'it is important that China's femaleness be unthreatening to the symbolic world of the film, so that she can come to represent law and order in small-town America' (1993: 25). Nonetheless Rothrock's genuine martial arts prowess again makes her an uncontainable body. Her ability to move around the scenery, to deliver kicks that drive her opponents around the screen, and her impression of compactness create a dynamism connoting the potential 'explosiveness' of a martial artist. This becomes the anticipated pleasure – the sudden break-out or counter-strike that comes to define the experience and becomes the measure of its energy.

It was precisely this that the post-classical action movie needed to re-inject a measure of conviction. It is perhaps with no coincidence that it was the mid-to-late 1990s, when Hong Kong was poised for its historic transition from British to Chinese control, that Asian stars and directors began to appear more fully integrated into the American film industry. In 1997, the year of the 'handover', John Woo directed possibly the most effective fusion of the American and Hong Kong styles in *Face/Off* (1997). The film bore stylistic and thematic resemblances to his 'heroic gunplay' films *Dip huet seung hung* (*The Killer*, 1989) and *Lat sau san taam* (*Hard Boiled*, 1992), not least in his copious deployment of slow motion to intensify moments of the kind of precise action associated with these films and the thematic preoccupation with the slippages of identity between cops and killers in a moral universe (religious imagery surfaces in most of his films).

The science fiction premise of having dedicated cop Sean Archer (John Travolta) swap his face (and, it would seem, his body shape) with that of psychotic gang leader Castor Troy (Nicholas Cage) to infiltrate his organisation is an excessively clear metaphor for the duality between cop and criminal, but it also provides a clear register of the perceived necessity to unbind the body (or the face, in this case) in order to permit this kind of thematic engagement to occur. With such an insane 'hook', the film's equally exaggerated emotional, psychological and thematic concerns become easier to accept without resorting to ironic distance.

Julian Stringer explores Woo's capacity to engage with these kinds of emotional registers that are 'so full of desire, anxiety and nostalgia. As narratives of machismo [they] do not have to be compromised' (1997: 33). By tracing the response to these films from Asian and American audiences, he points out, reinforcing Teo, Rodriguez and Williams, that within their culture of origin, the meanings of these films run to deeper genuine national and spiritual concerns but that on the aesthetic surface makes them available to Western audiences. *Face/Off* certainly plays to its exaggerations, but was not received as an exotic cult film. This was a major Hollywood release that found a broad audience. It is significant that that audience had just seen Cage engaged in the increasingly hysterical, purely American post-classical action films *The Rock* and *Con-Air*, making Woo's style seem controlled and coherent (which it is) by comparison.

Other Hong Kong directors were also working in Hollywood at this time, many with Jean-Claude Van Damme. Corey Yuen's *No Retreat, No Surrender* (1987), John Woo's *Hard Target* (1994), Ringo Lam's *Maximum Risk* (1996) and Tsui Hark's *Double Team* (1997) all feature the Belgian kickboxer, whose distinct combat style and toned athletic physique mark him as quite different from the hyperbolic hard bodies. Christine Holmlund analyses Van Damme's appeal as part of an overall exploration of the role of European actors in Hollywood action films. Interestingly, she notes that Van Damme himself credits his success with 'his willingness to get roughed up *and* be emotional' (2004: 291). In the terms outlined by Bordwell, this would make him a prefect vehicle for a Hong Kong director, and this may anecdotally explain his popularity with them.

Yet even Van Damme's trained body, capable of exceeding ordinary movement (playing characters who likewise continued to transcend rule systems in the name of redemptive action) was not enough. He was made into a cyborg in *Universal Soldier*, thrown through time in *Timecop* (1994) and duplicated in *Replicant* (2001) – exceeding the body's limits in an ever-more fantastical attempt to maintain agency against increasingly phantasmic opposition. The same was true of Jackie Chan, who following repeated attempts tried to break into the US market in preceeding decades, graduated to big-budget commercial mainstream American action films following the success of *Hung fan au* (*Rumble in the Bronx*, 1995). However, the actor's characteristic Buster Keaton-inspired martial arts style ultimately landed him in the role of the 'helper/buddy'. In the cop comedy *Rush Hour* (1998) he played sidekick to Chris Tucker doing a variant on Eddie Murphy's racial outsider defying criminal orthodoxy. Chan continued to fill these kinds of roles across two sequels to *Rush Hour* and both *Shanghai Noon* (2000) and *Shanghai Knights* (2003), ascending to fully-fledged lead in the children's film *The Tuxedo* (2002). What is interesting here is that the comic skill and timing that had signalled him as a distinct talent from Bruce Lee, became a marker of his infantilisation in Hollywood. In other words his explosive, frequently seemingly gravity-defying action remains bound.

Successful as these cross-overs were in generating box-office momentum and a whiff of the exotic, it was the more conventionally-rooted science fiction opus *The Matrix* that made the co-opting of the unbound body of the martial arts genre into a stylistically formalised element of the action palette. *The Matrix*, in some ways, completes the journey towards a wholly imaginary body begun in *Terminator 2: Judgment Day*. Just as the T-1000 in that film could not register injury and therefore became 'unstoppable' by virtue of superhuman abilities visualised through computer-generated imagery, so it should come as no surprise that the increasing sense of disconnection from the body and from reality would become the subject of several films at the turn of the millennium as well as an aspect of production methodology.

Andy Darley would describe the resulting epistemological effect as a 'second-order realism' (1997: 16), which he relates to the postmodern pre-

Second-order realism: Neo sees the world as it really is in *The Matrix* (1999)

cepts of the displacement of representation of social reality onto the representation of the process of representation itself. William Brown (2009) goes even further, arguing that digital technologies enable a truly posthumanist conception of cinema not only because of its capacity to render impossible bodies, but to create impossible viewpoints through simulated cameras with no challenging mechanical logistics. Importantly though, he remarks that the paradox of digital cinema is that its mode of address is, as Darley remarks, through realism: 'The depiction of the impossible has been a trait of cinema through its history. It is because digital cinema presents the impossible to us as if it were possible, rather, that it takes on its full posthumanist significance' (2009: 71).

On a similar note Thomas Wartenberg examines the 'deception hypothesis' (2005: 276) at the core of *The Matrix*, asking to what degree the film is illustrative of the philosophical question of the nature of our perception of reality with reference to a reality outside our perception – ie, if we believe the world to be real, is it real if there is no other reality outside of our perception of it? I have written elsewhere about this phenomenon in more general terms relating to millennial science fiction (see O'Brien 2002), but wish to briefly focus particularly on the paradox of self-erasure and self-negation represented by *The Matrix* as a post-classical action text, bearing in mind these few brief points.

The overall narrative trajectory of the *Matrix* trilogy is one of action in the philosophic sense we have engaged with throughout this book. It is a story of the volition and teleology of political revolution in which a character chooses to act in defiance of constraint and resistance with the ultimate aim of exceeding the limitations of the system that has failed him. In the first film Neo discovers his destiny to serve as a messiah for the enslaved human population, then struggles with self-doubt in *The Matrix Reloaded* (2003) before succeeding in bringing about the overthrow of machine control in *The Matrix Revolutions* (2003) through an act of self-sacrifice. In this respect *The Matrix* is an action film like any other. It embodies political and social action through combat, chase and other physical action. However, one of the central precepts of the entire trilogy is that the conflict is between a real and imagined universe.

The Matrix represents a kind of psychic screen (or 'second-order realism') which facilitates the repression of the human desire to resist oppression. This unreality is also what allows the characters to exceed the boundaries of human movement: seeming to move in slow motion, jump from impossible heights, and instantaneously acquire the knowledge and to apply martial arts training and perform 'superhuman' feats (choreographed by Hong Kong director Yuen Woo-Ping). This represents a paradox not unlike that facing most of the appropriation of Hong Kong precepts into mainstream Western films, in that it both releases and confines the body, freeing it from constraint, but only so far as an imaginary framework in which the illusory nature of that framework is a textual subject. This is an effect reminiscent of the uncomfortable double screening of reality in *Last Action Hero* and reframes the entire concept of social action within a reflexive formula that ultimately negates the status of that action as an act of will.

The Matrix was not the first film to explore this terrain in this period. Films including *The One* (2001) and even *Terminator 3: Rise of the Machines* navigated the waters of self-negation with storylines involving time travel and the paradox of wiping out your own identity with the potential salvation of mankind as the payoff. In all cases though, a restoration of self was really more at issue, and, in the case of *Terminator 3*, the freedom from constraint represented by a pre-determined (narratively or brand-identity-driven?) future. Frank Grady (2003) examines other films from the Schwarzenegger canon in terms of a narrative of sociopolitical amnesia corresponding with Schwarzenegger's attempt to refigure his identity. In *Total Recall* (1990) he portrays a quarry worker on Earth who may have been a double agent for the villainous ruler of Mars, and only uncovers the 'truth' when he volunteers for an implant that triggers his 'true' memories.

In *True Lies* (1994) he portrays a government specialist who hides his true identity from his wife and then must reconcile fact and fantasy when she suspects him of having an affair and becomes embroiled in a terrorist plot. In *Eraser* (1996) he is a government operative who specialised in protecting Federal witnesses by erasing any trace of their existence. The issue of erasure is entirely relevant to the trajectory of the classic action film throughout this period. As Grady concludes, 'doing the right thing means not only becoming a new person, long a traditional move in our exceptionalist and self-help-addicted culture, but also denying you were ever anybody else in the first place' (2003: 53).

It runs even deeper than this. At the end of *Total Recall* Quaid stands on the edge of a mountain on Mars with girlfriend Melina (Rachel Ticotin) on his arm staring at the dawn of a new planet where air is free to all, the population has been liberated from the tyrannical Vilos Cohaagen (Ronny Cox) and proof of alien life has been found. Quaid is struck by a terrible thought: what if this is all a dream? He was, after all, implanted with false memories at his own request. Unlike the nihilistic ending of *Brazil* (1985) where this is proved to be exactly the case and victim Sam Lowry (Jonathan Pryce) dreams of flight as he is dying on a torture chair, *Total Recall* leaves us in what may or may not be the fantasy in a surprisingly ambiguous moment of uplift.

This is exactly the paradox that places *The Matrix* firmly within the framework of a relativist, multicultural, postmodern, post-ideological America where self-determination is not so much an act of revolution or even an act of will – it is a choice, confined and constrained by a seemingly limitless but ultimately illusory perceptual framework. Anna Dawson makes the point that given the evidence that the collapse of civilisation was at least partly the fault of the humans, perhaps the machine evolution is the natural course of things and there is no reason why the audience should oppose their control. But, as she says, the point is that 'our ideological programming as it were would have the humans as worth saving' (2008: 32).

Given that the resolution of *The Matrix Revolutions* involves a choice for the humans between remaining in a new benign 'matrix' or in the rather grimy 'real' world, one wonders what Neo's sacrifice has ultimately solved. This is precisely the point – it has 'solved' nothing – it is merely a revelation of the nature of reality – a post-classical deconstruction of the ideologies behind the power structures that results in nothing more than a passive recognition of that fact. As Žižek notes in his reading of the films, for the series to work, it would have had to do nothing less than offer a real solution to the dilemma of the radical left – a real path to social transformation (which does not exist in this episteme): 'Capital is here to stay; all we can hope for is a temporary truce' (2009: 317).

At the climax of the first film, as noted previously, Neo finally realises this truth when he is able to 'read' the Matrix itself and 'see' his opponents as lines of computer code. It is a moment of genuine fusion of form and content in that it also reveals the state of the art of the posthumanist cinema. The film's bit of conceptual doggerel that defines the key to the perception of (false) reality – 'there is no spoon' – might easily be read as 'there is no body' or 'there is no ideology', thereby arguably addressing the audience to ask, as Neo does in a phone call to the computers controlling the Matrix at the end of the film, 'where do we go from here?': more precisely he says: 'I'm going to show them a world without you. A world without rules and controls, without borders or boundaries. A world where anything is possible. Where we go from there is a choice I leave to you.' Is the destiny of the action hero then now best understood not as the controlling volition of the *übermensch* but of that of a true liberator? Maybe, but as the twenty-first century drew on, the choices that defined us seemed surprisingly familiar. With 2001 as a traumatic flashpoint and the war in Iraq as a new Vietnam, the stage was set for the return of assurance.

4   THE RETURN

The Survival of Liberty

In *Die Hard With a Vengeance* (1995) John McClane faces the brother of Hans Gruber, the villain from the original film. Simon (Jeremy Irons) has begun a campaign of terrorist bombing in New York City, supposedly in reprisal for his brother's death. In reality, this is a front for yet another heist, robbing McClane of his dignity and agency with a deadly game while Gruber's mercenaries rob the Federal Reserve. In *Executive Decision*, Arab terrorists hijack a 747 and plan to release a deadly nerve gas over Washington DC. Elite commando Austin Travis (Steven Seagal) is dispatched to counter the threat, with academic analyst David Grant (Kurt Russell) in tow. When Travis dies unexpectedly early in the mission, Grant must respond by becoming the hero. In *The Siege* (1998) an Islamic terrorist cell wreaks havoc in New York City, forcing the government to introduce martial law, internment and torture to protect the citizenry.

In the wake of the terrorist attacks of 11 September 2001 in which 2,751 people were killed, it was presumed that the action film was finished forever. Few could imagine how these existing films could ever be shown again, let alone more films be made in that same mould. The withdrawal of *Collateral Damage* (2002), featuring Schwarzenegger as a firefighter seeking revenge on the Columbian terrorists who kill his family in an embassy bombing, was seen as a symbolic obituary. At a public forum on the role of cinema in national debate, New Line Cinema CEO Robert Shaye observed that 'What the world needs now is Hobbits' (see Traister *et al.* 2001), and the success of *The Lord of the Rings: The Fellowship of the Ring* and *Harry*

Potter and the Philosopher's Stone (2001) did seem to define the moment in popular cinema.

But *Collateral Damage* was released within four months of its initial withdrawal. According to the BBC Panorama documentary *A Warning From Hollywood* (2002), a group of American screenwriters, directors and producers including Steven De Souza (writer of *Die Hard* and *Die Hard 2*) and Lawrence Wright (writer of *The Siege*) was assembled for a three-day think tank at the request of the Pentagon to discuss the kinds of terrorist scenarios that could be (and indeed had been) imagined. Though in the same documentary former CIA Case Officer Robert Baer described this as 'idiotic... they should be having people with imagination in the government saying this is what we've got to do', when President George W. Bush addressed a joint session of Congress on 20 September 2001 he said: 'Tonight, we are a country awakened to danger and called to defend freedom. Our grief has turned to anger and anger to resolution. Whether we bring our enemies to justice or bring justice to our enemies, justice will be done' (2001).

Bush's call for the 'war on terror' came with an assertion of a global imperative to join this endeavour in the name of progress. He made the statement that America's (and the world's) enemies were 'the heirs of all the murderous ideologies of the twentieth century', suggesting a rejection of those ideologies and a new episteme in thought. The result, however, was as Stephen Prince discusses, the inauguration of the 'Terror Presidencies' (2009: 306), a phrase he derives from former Assistant Attorney General Jack Goldsmith. Motivated by fear, preoccupied by preemptive and preventative measures to defeat the threat of terror, leadership, government and the general citizenry finds itself in what Prince paraphases Jean-Paul Sartre by calling an 'untranscendable horizon of experience' (ibid.) that has a totalising character equivalent to conditions during the Cold War. This experience is described by many historians and cultural analysts including Susan Jacoby (2008), David Reynolds (2009) and Slavoj Žižek (2006, 2010) in terms of both neo-imperialism and religious and secular fundamentalism manifesting itself in the refiguration of a concept of totalising and largely anti-intellectual antagonism between righteousness and its other. Complex moral and ethical debates around nationality, culture and identity face reduction and simplification to a 'dumbed down' binary opposition in which, ironically, the 'choice' is no choice at all. The result is in a highly militarised culture of 'you are either with or against us' framed by the ethos of war ('support our troops') and an adherence to norms in which the teleology of action is framed by a sense of defense, protection and survival.

It is little wonder then that the action movie has come full circle during this episteme. Though calls for cinematic action did indeed shift register to both the fantastical (the continuing *Matrix* saga, the *Star Wars* prequels, superhero franchises) and the literal (the return of the war movie – *We Were Soldiers* (2002), *Jarhead* (2005), *The Hurt Locker* (2008)), the action film began to experience a rebirth by way of a return to its roots. This 'reboot', is, like other similar attempts to reinvent franchises and brands during the first decade of the twenty-first century, not exactly a process of total erasure or total recall, but rather, as the computer-derived term 'reboot' imputes, a dumping of faulty or non-functional operating systems without damaging long-term memory.

The neo-classical action movie demonstrates a reaction against the displacement, relativism, illusionism and increasingly plastic unreality of the post-classical period by a return to 'old school' virtues of deci-sive reaction to threats and traumas and a renewed commitment to the physicality of action. In *The Expendables* aged mercenary Barney Ross (Sylvester Stallone) engages a team of elite warriors to take down a dictator backed by a shady ex-CIA agent. Throughout the film a cast of 1980s action icons including Stallone, Willis, Schwarzenegger, Dolph Lundgren and Eric Roberts appear, sometimes debating the merits of experience and the dolours of age with a cast of more recent action stars, some of them already also iconic including Jason Statham, Jet Li, Steve Austin and Randy Couture. The 2012 sequel would even include appearances by Jean-Claude Van Damme and Chuck Norris.

It is difficult to look at *The Expendables* without context. We are reminded of it with every step. Its narrative trajectory is classical: mercenaries go where no one else will to take down a nemesis no one else can; not just because they're paid to, but because they must – if they do not, the beauti-ful freedom-fighting daughter of the evil dictator will die at the hands of the waterboarding rogue CIA agent. The stain of covert intervention is erased by the surgical application of violence to overthrow the unjust and purge the undesirable elements of the American self, externalised in the nemesis.

The film is also physically grounded in the roots of the genre on the level of execution. It is a consciously 'back to basics' presentation of action in action, eschewing CGI and wirework for hardcore combat, a fact made clear by the publicity campaign surrounding Stallone's neck injury sustained during shooting while in combat with Steve Austin. Stallone's direction emphasises the power of physical blows upon the body, intercutting sweaty close-ups and bloody action with reaction shots that are again testament to the physicality with which these scenes have been mounted. The image of Stallone striking the wall that broke his neck remains in the film, and produces the sympathetic kinesthetic wince you would expect.

The effect of this renewed commitment to the physicality of action, together with its consequences (wounds, injuries, violent and up-close-and-personal death and torture) speaks to the culture of 'old-school' fundamentalism where direct action – war, vengeance, punching or kicking someone in reprisal for an attack – necessitates an experiential, kinesthetic sensation for cathartic effect. The question, as Žižek (2006) asks, is of the meaning and the context of this return, or, in terms of the philosophy of action, what is its teleology?

Žižek explores the philosophical precept of the eternal return in the context of debates on religion and politics, with reference to Lacan, Nietzsche, Heidegger and Benjamin. Without wanting to get drawn into a debate with that company, it is worth summarising Žižek's basic question on the topic of 'the return', which he poses relative to the context of human progress in the post-human age. To what degree, he asks, does technological evolution (such as digitalisation) and the migration of contexts (debates on the post-human) over time represent a movement away from the patterns of the past and to what degree are they merely a revisiting of them? He asks: 'Does it stand for the factual repetition, for the repetition of the past which should be willed as it was, or for a Benjaminian repetition, a return-reactualisation of that which was lost in the past occurrence, of its virtual excess, of its redemptive potential?' (2006: 193). If we apply this question to the 'return' embodied in the neo-classical action film, the same issue is at stake – is there a process of 'reactualisation' wherein the social and political context lost in the excess of the spectacularisation can be revisited in a new context, or is this merely a repeating of the pattern with a new aesthetic 'skin'?

The 'reboot' of the James Bond franchise is an interesting case in this context, although the Bond 'adventures' are more properly suited to a discussion of the colonialist adventure movie where Bond, as the servant of Empire, represents its interests first and foremost (with two notable exceptions before the 'reboot': *On Her Majesty's Secret Service* (1969) in which the personal becomes paramount when Bond takes a wife; and *Licence to Kill* (1989) in which Bond pursues an unofficial vendetta against a drug lord and is disavowed by MI6). It is significant that *Die Another Day* (2002), the last film in the ironic and postmodern Brosnan cycle, had featured extensive computer-generated effects, including a major stunt involving a cliff dive by the character Jinx (Halle Berry) that was clearly digitally rendered, removing all trace of potential kinesthetic connection with the actions on screen.

Casino Royale bore the stylistic hallmarks not of the exotic adventures of the past, but of a restorative, regenerative and energetic sense of the power of Bond as an agent (in every sense) by exploring how he 'became' one. There is a strong emphasis on Bond (Daniel Craig) being tested at all times: a driven, energetic and dangerous energy in or out of a vehicle, armed or unarmed, but one never quite in control. All of this evinces in the perceived necessity to keep a young and genuinely physical actor in frame and in motion and to achieve greater intensity through photography and editing to emphasise the impact of blows and kicks rather than simply editing for the sake of 'bustle'. This is particularly marked during the brutal pre-credit sequence depicting a bloody, destructive battle in a public restroom where a man's head is smashed against a porcelain sink, which shatters.

Linda Williams does not address the action film in her writing on body genres because at the time of her writing the action film had yet to develop this kind of visual intensity, however her analysis of the psychoanalytic interconnection with the empathetic (and mimetic) experience of film viewing is relevant. She describes genres requiring a high degree of involvement in sensation (horror, pornography, melodrama) as lacking 'aesthetic distance' (1991: 5). Such films, she argues emphasise up-close-and-personal depiction of moments registering the body 'caught in the grip of intense sensation or emotion' (ibid.) with the focus on 'what could probably best be called a form of ecstasy' (ibid.). This is descriptive of the intensified aesthetic of the neoclassical action movie, which can clearly be seen as a 'reactualisation' of the genre – a restoration of the qualities of kinesthesia in narratives depicting decisive (reactive) volitionism.

The Bourne Identity (2002) was central in foregrounding a restorative aesthetic of physicality and action in action. The first of three in a cycle continuing with *The Bourne Supremacy* (2004) and concluding with *The Bourne Ultimatum* (2007), it pursued an overall narrative trajectory of survival, resistance and revenge underscored by a narrative of restoration as amensiac black-ops agent Jason Bourne (Matt Damon) recovers his true identity while enduring the loss of his capacity to forge a new one because of the relentless pursuit of governmental forces who perceive him to be a threat. The Bourne films consciously deglamourised and reactualised the espionage genre by an emphasis on defining rather than stylising physical detail in depicting the environment – places where action could occur in spaces that facilitated the dynamics of action itself rather than serve as a picturesque backdrop, an increased use of hand-held 'shaky-cam' shooting to capture dynamic motion in close-up during scenes of combat, and featured extensive chases both on foot and in vehicles that emphasised physical authenticity through explicit, visible damage and injury to property and person. All of this is set against a narrative of personalised vengeance framed by a quest for restoration – Bourne seeking to 'claim his life back' with extreme prejudice.

It is precisely this sense of intensity that Prince identifies as underlying the return of the vigilante film as a way of 'coding and transposing' (2009: 287) the rage and trauma of 9/11. Links with contemporary moral debates around ethics, torture and militarisation were often quite explicit in films like *A History of Violence* (2005), *The Brave One, Taken, Outlaw* (2007), and *Death Sentence* (2007). Like their predecessors in the urban western (there has even been talk of a *Death Wish* remake), in each of the films the actions of the protagonists are justified by acts of outrage or offence to which there is a motivated, post-traumatic and justifiable response.

Death Sentence (based on the original sequel novel to *Death Wish*) has closer affiliations with the horror genre to which director James Wan made a defining contribution with *Saw* (2004), where torture as a fantasy motif had all-too-clear resonance with the appearance of images of real-life torture in Abu Ghraib and Guantánamo. The image of the traumatised hero Nick Hume (Kevin Bacon) engaged in a self-destructive spiral of vengeance with the killers of his son ends in an orgiastic bloodbath. Horror veteran David Cronenberg likewise finds the vigilante frame an apt register for his characteristic motifs of mutation and the abjection of the repressed internal other as mild-mannered diner-owner Tom Stall (Viggo Mortensen) is revealed to be a mafia assassin capable of acts of extreme, explosive and bloody violence amid a sombre, reflective study of the core values of the American family.

Taken is more generically action-oriented in following the furious and urgent pursuit of kidnappers who have taken the daughter of a CIA operative Bryan Mills (Liam Neeson). Like *Casino Royale* or *Bullitt* before it the film deploys an aesthetic of close observation of the subject in constant motion, charting and recording each bruising, brutal encounter with every link in the human traffic chain. Again the paradox of necessity and volition drives the characterisation of this hero – he is trained to act and chooses to respond. Again, however, this vigilante is shown to be antiheroic and socially irredeemable – disenfranchised from his daughter's affection following a divorce he is compelled to save her but doomed to remain without reconstitution within the family, the events of *Taken 2* (2012) notwithstanding, where franchise logic compelled the absent feminine counterpart to become present in the form of Famke Janssen as Mills' estranged wife, requiring a redemptive rescue.

Another, more grandiose, more extreme and even more visually extravagant vengeance narrative to attain broad cultural purchase at this time was *Kill Bill* (a single film divided into two parts for distribution purposes: for the sake of simplicity, let's just call it *Kill Bill*). Here Quentin Tarantino presents an homage to Asian action films, liberally read in terms of exemplary postmodernism. In it a character called The Bride (Uma Thurman), formerly part of a team of elite assassins, tracks down members of her unit who have betrayed her and kills each in turn, leading her, in time, to their leader, Bill (David Carradine), whom she also kills. Like all Tarantino films, *Kill Bill* seems calculated to provoke both scholarly and fanboy analysis, and certainly touches a number of key registers of the genre. Equally though the film becomes a point of focus in terms of its numerous conscious transgressions of representational taboos, among them numerous acts of brutality against women, many of them enacted by women, and in its avowed aim of stripping the genre down to its purest core – action and reaction.

The film contains scene after scene of combat, conflict, attack, response, escape – all of it following an overall trajectory of survival, resistance and revenge that represents a process of 'cleansing' of corruption by The Bride, be it the hypersaturated postmodernism of O-Ren Ishii's (Lucy Liu) Tokyo or the mock Zen presented by Bill himself. Both are seen to be inauthentic and overdetermined, and both are erased by The Bride. Of her opponents, only Elle Driver (Daryl Hannah) is shown to be as uncluttered by cultural bricolage, but her motivations are portrayed as corrupt and selfish. She therefore represents a derangement of the righteousness represented by The Bride and must also be exterminated.

The universe of *Kill Bill* is so laden with seemingly miscellaneous intertextual detritus as to prove a distraction from its really rather rudimentary centre, and yet there, at its centre is the single thread of the pursuit of vengeance and the purpose that it serves that unites all of these vigilante narratives, which, in Tarantino's terms, is the core summative experience of the cinema of action in the first place – something of the 'ecstasy' of which Williams wrote (1991: 5). This is coming, it should be remembered, from the sensibility of a *cineaste* avowedly defined by cinephilia: as Howard Hampton puts it: 'imposing a devout connoisseur's attitude on long, sticky strings of cult and exploitation-film platitudes' (2005: 53). Geoffrey O'Brien is rather more kind in pointing out that what makes *Kill Bill* effective is exactly this artificiality and formalism. He notes: 'The air of flagrant artifice must be sustained, in the first place, to prevent any apprehension that the violence is real' (2003: 25). This cannot really be said of the other post 9/11 vigilante films, and yet the generic framework in evidence in these films threatens to muddy the waters of ethical engagement where as Henry Giroux remarks, there is 'the need to accentuate the tension between the growing threat to public life and the promise of a democracy that both remembers the history of human suffering and works to prevent its reoccurrence' (2002: 284).

Vigilantism is taken to this level of explicitly political, ethical and historical context in *Munich*, where a team of Israeli agents is sent on a mission to kill the Arab terrorists responsible for the 1972 Olympic massacre. The film is intertextual with the 'evil Arab' action movies of the 1980s and 1990s to the extent that the overarching political dynamic is exactly the same, and likewise the narrative structure and characterisation is alarmingly close to the classic mercenary/vigilante plot of covert, illegitimate intervention to right societal wrongs irresolvable by diplomacy in the face of an intractable nemesis and a deal more subtle than the equivalent line in *The Bourne Legacy* (2012) where Retired Colonel Eric Byer (Edward Norton) describes black ops as 'morally indefensible and absolutely necessary'.

Like in *The A-Team*, moral justification is sought through citation: in that case Gandhi, in this Israeli Prime Minister Golda Meir. Though Avner (Eric Bana), the team leader, has his doubts about what is, essentially an act of murderous vengeance and not a legitimate military action, he is assured by Meir (Lynn Cohen) that 'every civilisation finds it necessary to negotiate compromises with its own values'. This is a fictive line of dialogue from the mouth of an historical personage in a film made in a dramatic register by a filmmaker with credits both in fantastical and realistic modes of address, but it is entirely descriptive of the morality at the heart of the action film as ethical trope.

In terms of their 'readability' within the framework of then contemporary moral and political debate, these films offer complications of *realpolitik* crosscurrents. *Munich* may be the most transparent, with its straightforward assertion of the moral dilemma at the core of its narrative – how far can you go in the name of national security and to what extent is that security defined necessarily by your capacity for violent reprisal against your enemies? Reynolds warns that the natural corollary to this process, in which a framing of a fundamentalist (and increasingly religious) stoicism in terms of the image of freedom for all (as defined by the Imperial centre) is the culture of conversion. He speaks of the image of a 'Crusader State' (2009: 583), an historical simile not infrequently evoked during the Iraq War, and his book is aptly titled *America, Empire of Liberty*. Tim Jon Semmerling (2006) examines the 'evil Arab' paradigm in terms of an old-fashioned model of Orientalism, whereby the ideological discomfort at the heart of this dynamic is reflective of as simultaneous fascination and abjection with the 'other' that reflects instabilities at the core of what appears a dominant orthodoxy in the first place. In other words the totalising ethos of the age of terror is very much a grounding teleology for a reactive ethic of action tragically blind to its inevitable cyclicality.

The conclusion of *Munich* frames haunted, paranoid Avner, torn by angst following the success of his mission, against the Manhattan skyline, complete with the Twin Towers of the World Trade Center. This makes explicit the association between this historical act of vengeance and the legacy of vengeance as an element of historical process. The implication is obvious – a cycle of violence never ends and every action leads to a reaction, which in turn leads to another action and so on. In the climate of 2005 when the film was released, this was impossible to ignore as a

The legacy of terror: Munich (2005)

question posed by this story told at this time, also intertextual with even deeper political issues surrounding the ethics of this act of vengeance relative to discourses around the Holocaust – is all subsequent Israeli violence morally justifiable as a 'preventative war' against further anti-Semitic genocide, and to what extent it this reflective of the paradoxes of American neoimperialism framed as the righteous preservation of democracy? What may have been easier to miss in the light of this explicit political resonance as far as *Munich* is concerned are the roots of both the question and the form of the story within the framework of an action film, but that is exactly what it is: a reactive tale of the restoration of agency through the decisive application of violence in which the bulk of the 'action' centres on acts of specific violence (the assassinations) which make explicit that action has been and is being taken to see 'justice' done, just as George W. Bush had called for.

Old Guys

In *RED* (2010) former black-ops agent Joe Matheson (Morgan Freeman) speaks with old friend and colleague Frank Moses (Bruce Willis) at the retirement home where Matheson now resides. 'Vietnam, Afghanistan, Green Springs Rest Home' says Matheson wrly. The one enemy that got him, he notes, is the one he never saw coming – age. Yet age does not prevent the 'Retired: Extremely Dangerous' team from having a fully-fledged adventure in the subsequent movie, nor did it appear to be an impediment to John Rambo and John McClane, both of whom resurfaced in the mid-

2000s in very belated sequels that significantly reconstituted their heroes in the framework of reactualisation and return.

Perhaps the answer to the conundrum of the return is to be found, ironically, in post-classicism itself, where the intertextuality of many of these films retains links with postmodern and post-classical deconstructionism and reflexivity. This implies, as Elsaesser and Buckland (2002) note, a degree of engagement by the audience with the text as text, which they read intertextually with other films of the kind. Few audiences came to *Die Hard 4.0* and *Rambo* unaware of their predecessors. Likewise, it would be difficult to watch *The Expendables* without understanding the iconic resonance of its cast, combining old stars and new in an avowedly reconstitutive artifice, or likewise to appreciate either the popular acclaim and affection afforded to *Rocky Balboa* (2006) as a mirror of Stallone's commitment to a much-loved character.

More than 50 per cent of the poster advertising for *The Expendables* was taken up with the names of nine of the principal cast. One tagline read 'Every movie has a hero. This one has them all.' Though Wilis and Schwarzenegger play minor roles, the uniting of the three principal investors in Planet Hollywood is itself a moment of meta-history. Ever the most nimbly subversive of the three as a performer, Willis gets to undercut the machismo of the confrontation between Stallone and Schwarzenegger as rival mercenary commanders bidding for his contract with the line 'So, are you two going to start sucking each other's dicks now?' a line Stallone claims was ad-libbed in rehearsal.

The secondary casting is probably even more significant. *The Expendables* is highly conscious that the action movie has evolved, and that new stars have emerged, even if they do not represent the kind of broad iconographic cultural presence and box-office earning represented by Stallone, Willis and Schwarzenegger in their heyday. The bulk of the action in the film (together with the hysterically heterosexual romantic subplot) is carried by Jason Statham, the lean, shaven-headed British actor who emerged first from British gangster films *Lock, Stock and Two Smoking Barrels* (1998) and *Snatch* (2000), replete with their cultural associations with the 'new laddism' of the 1990s, before achieving transnational action hero status in the French-produced Corey Yuen-directed *The Transporter* (2002). Here he assumed the legacy of Steve McQueen as a driver for hire whose ability to command a vehicle corresponds with his command of self (and society – he makes a moral choice to defy criminals who hire him to transport a kidnap victim). Statham is *The Expendables'* principal actor beside Stallone, and there is a fascinating dynamic of master/apprentice at work that ironically would be played out in 2011 with Statham taking the Charles Bronson role in the remake of *The Mechanic* (1972).

Jet Li, who had co-starred with Statham in *War* (2007) was, as previously noted, an established Hong Kong action star before belatedly arriving in Hollywood as an exotic object to be mocked and contained in *Lethal Weapon 4* (1998): 'enter the drag queen' quips Riggs when his character appears in traditional Chinese dress. Elements of that characterisation remain here in the repeated gags about the character's height, but Li underplays his scenes in an effectively matter-of-fact way that gives him the capacity to sustain and ignore the textual and thematic jibes thrown at him from the privileged white centre.

Dolph Lundgren may have seemed the most surprising choice of star, but the Swedish actor had made a significant comeback in the preceeding years with direct-to-DVD films including *The Mechanik* (2005) and *Missionary Man* (2007) in which he had demonstrated not only an enduring physical presence, but a fairly capable directorial hand, rendering classic 'old school' mercenary and vengeance narratives. Randy Couture and Steve Austin represent the crossover between sports entertainment and action movies that also characterised the direct-to-video years. Austin was a professional wrestler, and already had several low-budget action credits to his name. Couture was a mixed martial arts Ultimate Fighting Champion (UFC) fighter, and it is no accident that Stallone has their characters face off in a brutal encounter at the film's climax where the intense, actual physicality of the two men was given expression against an elemental conflagration of burning fuel.

Stallone's sense not only of his own history, but of the contours of the genre as it had evolved is evident here, and the sense of historical intertextuality is central to the audience's experience. The same is true of *Rocky Balboa*. When the aging but still determined Rocky faces off against angry young champion Mason 'The Line' Dixon (Antonio Tarver), who has been goaded into the fight by dint of (significantly) a computer simulation which predicted Rocky would win, Rocky responds to Dixon's trash-talk with 'There ain't nothing over 'til it's over.' Dixon creases his brow skeptically and says 'Where's that from, the eighties?' to which Rocky responds after a brief pause: 'That's probably the seventies.' Audiences who had endured Rocky's underdog struggles since 1976 could not but feel warm nostalgia represented by this (verbal, soon to be physical) confrontation. But when confronted by the dialogue in and tagline for *Rambo* – 'Live for nothing, or die for something' (replaced in some territories by the rather bland but still descriptive 'Heroes Never Die: They Just Reload'), feelings of discomfort were the general result. However, audiences might also have done well to pay attention to another key line from *Rocky Balboa*, equally unapologetic in its unreconstructed hardbody heroism – 'it ain't about how hard you hit, it's about how hard you can *get* hit and keep moving forward', an apt summary of both Stallone's career and the philosophy of the action film.

In this double recognition of intertextual and metatextual signifiers, we may see something of a solution to the reconciliation of the overload associated with the postmodern and the meaning of 'the return'. The selectivity of the viewing experience and its intertextuality not with other films applies not just to aesthetics and patterns, but with the cognitive and intellectual experience of viewing other films in an increasingly obvious (and foregrounded) sociopolitical context. Larry Knapp (2008) writes of this with particular reference to intertextuality in *Domino* (2005). Knapp charts the progress of director Tony Scott from the 'high concept' years of *Top Gun* (1986) and *Days of Thunder* (1990) through the post-classical stylings of *The Last Boy Scout* (1991) and *True Romance* (1993) arguing that in the post-millennium he transgressed even the post-classical to arrive not at neo-classicism, but what he terms 'hyperclassicism'.

In films like *Man on Fire* (2004), *Domino* and *Deja Vu* (2006), Knapp argues that Scott deploys the hyperstimulated aesthetic of the postmodern blockbuster not as a mystification, but as a means to enable what he calls a 'concentrated subjectivity' (ibid.). In this he means that the deployment of intertextuality and disjunctive filming and editing techniques concentrates the sense of the film experience *as film*. This undermines the delusion hypothesis and forces the audience to engage with the representations they see as representation, and yet continue to feel empathetic responses precisely *because* of the imagistic stimulation. Thus, he says the audience cannot ignore 'the irrevocable loss of continuity, and the status of the image not as a synergistic decoration of digital simulacrum, but as a symptom and agent of cultural flux and despair' (ibid.). In this *Domino* navigates both the real life of bounty-hunter Domino Harvey and the media-saturated environment in which she operated, mirrored in the film's relentless reference to the 'mediation' surrounding the character.

Could the same be argued of the various films featuring increasingly aging action stars that appeared in the millennial decade? Reviewing *JCVD* (2008), a singular art-house/action movie crossover starring Jean-Claude Van Damme, in the *New York Times* A. O. Scott asked: 'What does an aging action-movie superstar have to do to keep himself in the game? The real world choices are limited. Keep going, oblivious to the ravages of time, in the pathologically stoical manner of Sylvester Stallone. Embrace self-parody and character roles in indie films, as Bruce Willis has so brilliantly done. Maybe become the governor of a large state, or, failing that, a tough-talking cheerleader for Mike Huckabee' (2008).

Most of this quotation is clear enough, but, just to clarify, the reference to cheerleading for Mike Huckabee refers to Chuck Norris, who in 2008 endorsed the fundamentalist candidate Mike Huckabee in his bid for the Republican Presidential nomination. He also published a book of his political views entitled *Black Belt Patriotism: How to Reawaken America* in which he expounded on the importance of recalling the founding traditions of American patriotic idealism, making him as apt a icon of neoconservative fundamentalism as he was hardbody American neo-westernism, again raising the question of to what extent these are one in the same thing.

JCVD is a European co-production shot in Belgium in which Jean-Claude Van Damme plays 'himself'; an aging action third-rank movie star (struggling to win parts in low-budget films but losing out to Steven Seagal) in the middle of a nasty divorce and custody process that has left him short of funds. A fateful visit to a local post office finds him in the midst of a *Dog Day Afternoon* robbery and hostage scenario (one of the robbers even vaguely resembles John Cazale). When a shot is fired through the window, locals and police do not know what is going on inside, but they do know Van Damme went in there because he had just spoken with some adoring fans who run a local video store, and so assume, because of his well-publicised personal problems, that he is robbing the place. Drama ensures inside and out as Van Damme balances the image of hero, villain and ordinary person, including some soul-searching dialogue scenes where he wrestles with elements of his real-world demons (divorce, drugs, career choices).

JCVD is a remarkably reflexive film, but given its European roots, more in the mould of Jean-Luc Godard than *Last Action Hero*. It opens with an extended parody of the hyperbolic action movie in which, seemingly in one take, Van Damme kicks, punches, rolls and battles his way through a firefight and dispatches numerous opponents. This is shown to be a film on which he is working and getting no respect from the Asian director (who is throwing darts at a target with 'Hollywood' written on it). It reflects upon the action film, but also the figure of the action hero, particularly in terms of the schism between his capacity to act and the impression of a capacity to act created by film as a medium.

The film's structure frustrates straightforward narrative by way of disrupting the chain of causality associated with the enacting of will. Events are not as they appear, and parts of the plot are revealed in an elliptical fashion, allowing the film to fill in significant character detail that does not advance the 'action' much but does advance the themes and characterisation. It also oscillates between scenes in which Van Damme appears to be active or in action in either negotiating or even fighting, and scenes that show this is frequently an illusion and that he is, in reality, completely constrained by the circumstances.

This is a key point, and the film rather poignantly allows Van Damme space to expound on these things in dialogue allegedly at least partly improvised. In turn, he allows French-Algerian director Mabrouk El Mechri to film him in sepia tones which emphasise the actor's craggy, worn, make-up free features, demonstrating the ravages of time and lifestyle upon the person behind the icon. This is most pointed in an extended monologue delivered directly to camera where Van Damme is literally lifted out of the scenery of the movie and into the rafters where lighting rigs are

Mistakes I have made: Jean-Claude Van Damme as Jean-Claude Van Damme in *JCVD* (2008)

visible and he reflects directly on the mistakes in his life and career.

The film is still a fiction, of course (Van Damme's real-life custody battle was over his son, but in the film it is a daughter, and, obviously enough, this is not a real robbery) and the film enjoys its reference to mediation, not least in its opening scene where the Arab video store owners debate the representation of Arabs in *The Delta Force* and other action films. The climax also presents Knapp's 'concentrated subjectivity' with a doubled resolution in which, when Van Damme is dragged from the post office at gunpoint, the film begins to 'judder' at the edges of the frame as if there were a problem in projection. This triggers a fantasy register where in the idiom of his action roles, Van Damme spins, kicks and disarms his opponent, then high-fives a nearby member of the SWAT team. The film then 'judders' back to its 'reality' mode where he, rather unglamorously, elbows the man in the stomach and falls to the ground long enough for the police to close in both on the gunman and on Van Damme, whom they handcuff and jostle into a waiting police car.

JCVD is fairly singular in its level of indexical interconnection with reality, but the basic dynamic of examining the nature and role of the hero against the constraints of age and obsolescence intertextual with the age of the stars is a common theme in several of the films of this period, particularly those offered as a 'capping' (or maybe a reboot) of their franchises: *Die Hard 4.0* and *Rambo*. In many ways the entire *Die Hard* series pursues this theme against a backdrop of the perceived obsolescence of the blue-collar white male in the face of a changing (bureaucratic, corporate, affluent, Japanese-colonised) society. As Neal King puts it: 'Cops have just a few talents to share; they know how to identify, catch, and kill evil men. They believe these talents to be in unaccountably low demand, and of course they would rather find a market for their labour than let it slip into disuse' (1999: 40). King examines how the dynamics of any cop film set up an opposition between managerial classes (bosses, commissioners, captains, mayors, etc) and the frontline cop, and how this allows the alignment of the white male hero with the oppressed underclasses rather that the patriarchal centre.

In *Die Hard*, McClane's stubborn adherence to old-fashioned ideals was contrasted with his wife's success in the corporate world which has also inspired the film's villains. Meanwhile Bruce Willis's transition from smart-alec television star to action hero informed part of the film's post-classical context in that the 'wink to the audience' factor played a part in the empathy he inspired. In *Die Hard 2* McClane's refusal to obey jurisdiction and hierarchies means he is able to elude both the airport authorities and the ersatz soldiers who prove to be amoral mercenaries. It also played upon the 'superstar' status of both McClane (in the film) and Willis (as star) by dealing with how his celebrity ('how can the same shit happen to the same guy twice?') plays a role in the terrorist's plot. This was further amplified in *Die Hard With a Vengeance*. His 'broken down' status (wife now gone, McClane is washed up and off duty) is seen to be sufficient reason to assume that Simon Gruber's (Jeremy Irons) campaign of vendetta has no ulterior motive other than revenge, even though this is not true. Also, in being such a belated entry in the series, Willis's own status as an action hero actor was subject to some measure of reflection in the characterisation.

This pattern is repeated in *Die Hard 4.0*. Inspired by a piece of journalism on cyberterrorism in *Wired* magazine by John Carlin, it literally pits old-school muscle and guts against technology as McClane battles a cyberterrorist attack. The film visually oscillates between scenes of action and confrontation set in the high-gloss up-world of the technological society and McClane's sometimes unexpected use of the space and its objects ('you killed a helicopter with a car') in a more manually-intensive and 'basic' manner. As in all three previous films, McClane's capacity to access the industrial underbelly of the edifices of progress (the heating ducts and building spaces of the Nakatomi tower, the service areas of Dulles airport, the sewers of New York) represents a physical and psychic connection between McClane and the 'earth' – the 'ground' – the rooted 'common soil' of America from which he constantly finds himself removed but must return to in order to regain the upper hand. In terms of its broader ideological context, this restating of the class dilemma of the working male, now aging, technologically-challenged and embodied by a visibly aging actor is doubled in political currency simply by dint of its US title – *Live Free or Die Hard* which explicitly expresses the binary opposition of the period – 'with us or against us'.

Žižek speaks of this, pointing out that the 'choice' of allegiance is not a matter of evaluation when framed against a society that is simply not given enough information with which to make an educated decision. He remarks that in contrast to the twentieth century's ideological struggles of the Cold War and against European Fascism, where the 'other' was both real and identifiable 'the terrorist threat is inherently spectral, without a visible centre', and that 'the paradoxical result of this spectralisation of the enemy is an unexpected reversal: in this world without a clearly defined Enemy, it is the USA itself, the protector against the threat, which is emerging as a main enemy' (2006: 374). In these terms *Die Hard 4.0* presents a division between two versions of America – the aging hard body and the emerging digital paradigm, and argues that under the latter will always lie the former, and that the application of decisive strength will always be the best defense.

Rambo engages a similar set of expectations not least in it simply being a *Rambo* film. Though John McClane may have limped partially into the 1990s, Rambo was firmly seen as an icon of the 1980s. Though as noted a warm, fuzzy glow greeted the return of Rocky Balboa, Stallone's pathological stoicism (to paraphrase Scott) was seen as a liability when it came to resurrecting this particular character. In the event, *Rambo* represents a very pure, very direct neo-classical action movie, depicting action as action with full commitment to explicit viscerality and without concession to relativism or reflexivity (even *Rambo III* winked to the audience). It is an unreconstructed tale of the necessity to take action in the face of evil, in this case Burma (Myanmar), a political hotspot in reality, where its ruling military Junta had come under increasing scrutiny in the 2000s around human and civil rights abuses.

The plot revolves around a team of religious aid workers who elicit Rambo's reluctant help as an escort into Burma, but become trapped there and subject to abuse by a brutal Burmese military officer (who is also a homosexual pederast). The film's skepticism with diplomacy and charity work is explicit, with the well-meaning but naive missionaries ultimately falling afoul of the forces of social control in what is shown to be an inherently corrupt regime. In the classic tradition of the cinema of action, in this situation the only solution is direct action, which is what Rambo takes, albeit with the necessary support of mercenaries he manages to persuade through force of arms that they need to help too.

Rambo is by far the most explicitly gory of all the films in the series, with Stallone in interviews remarking that if horror films like *Saw* and *Hostel* (2005) are tolerated, it should be equally acceptable to represent violence as graphically in his films. This calls to mind Williams' analysis of the body genres and the question of intensity and ecstasy. *Rambo* is the very epitome of this paradigm in the action film. With Stallone consciously citing neoconservative horror films as precedent, the circle is complete. The result is gruesome disembowelments, throat-slashings and an astonishing scene depicting the disintegration of Burmese soldiers by machine gun which, though naturally the product of cutting-edge make-up effects, make the representation of action and its consequences for the body in the film considerably more difficult to accommodate within a broad fantasy register than the gunplay in *The Matrix* or even *Rambo: First Blood Part II*. It certainly exceeds Prince's (2003) metaphysical paradox of the inanimate body in (re)action, as the Burmese soldiers do not so much twitch in death as liquefy under the power of the gun. Likewise in *The Expendables*, a Somali pirate (intertextual with both the reality of twenty-first century piracy and the *Pirates of the Caribbean* adventure series?) is literally torn in half by a gunshot from a powerful weapon: death is not a spectacle – it is an erasure.

Possibly the most important motif in *Rambo*, though, is of regeneration. Yes this is inherent in the standard narrative convention of a reluctant hero rising to the challenge after an initial period of refusal, and this has been the core narrative of all of the sequels to *First Blood*. It also lies at the heart of *The Expendables*, connoted both in the restoration of aim in the Statham character with which the film concludes and in the slightly deeper resonance of locating the heroes' club house in New Orleans. However, a more significant and specific restoration or renewal of spirit occurs for *Rambo* in this film in that his association with the missionary Sarah (Julie Benz) rejuvenates his sense of patrimonial and familial values.

Though in *Rambo: First Blood Part II* Co represented something of a romantic interest for Rambo (an armed and skilled Vietnamese fighter who contributes to his escape from torture, then, after exchanging a necklace as a mark of friendship, is killed), Rambo's feelings for Sarah are shown to be more fatherly in nature. Having failed to 'protect' Co (which was never his job), he chooses to protect Julie, and in so doing rejuvenates Rambo's sense of family and home (and arguably his humanity). This prompts his repatriation at the end of the film, a literal 'coming home' in which, to the strains of the song 'It's a Long Road' from *First Blood*, Rambo walks along a country road in the United States towards a farm in the distance where the name on the letter box at the gate reads 'Rambo'. At the time of writing, a fifth film is planned, currently said to involve a domestic rather than a foreign battle for Rambo to fight, which would bring the series completely back to its roots as a tale of dissent in America. The possibilities for such a film have been limited though, by both Stallone's continuation of *The Expendables* franchise and the critically and commercially unsuccessful remake of *Straw Dogs* (2011) which relocates the action to the US and makes its pacifist expatriate mathematician into a Hollywood screenwriter facing troubles with atavistic Southerners in rural Mississippi.

Regeneration is also at the heart of *Terminator: Salvation*, also a reboot following the lacklustre and largely ignored *Rise of the Machines*. The wisdom of such a move seems evasive other than in the context of the industrial imperative for brand-driven franchise productions equally evinced by the ongoing *Expendables*, *Taken*, and *Die Hard* brands, as well as the essentially uncalled for remakes *Total Recall* (2012), *Red Dawn* (2012) and *Robocop* (2013). Thomas Schatz observes that in economic terms Millennial Hollywood was dominated by, in his estimation, two dozen active film franchises plus another dozen or so single film franchises. He remarks: 'The franchise mentality has intensified during the conglomerate era, and in the new millennium it has gone into another register altogether due to the combined effects of digitisation and media convergence, which have significantly impacted both production and formal-aesthetic proto-cols, and due also to the effects of globalisation as Hollywood fashions its top films for a worldwide marketplace' (2009: 30).

Yet *Terminator: Salvation* is also a clear product of the visual palette of the Iraq War, with its dried and dusty landscapes photographed seemingly through a heat haze resembling nothing of the flash-forward future from the previous films. The film is kinetic, certainly, featuring seemingly endless scenes of action, and yet though at one point resembling more a reboot of *Mad Max 2* than *The Terminator* (complete with 'feral' ethnic child and a truck crashing along a debris-strewn post-apocalyptic highway), it never actually generates momentum. Its 'heavy lies the crown' plotline surrounding John Connor's (Christian Bale) doubts about precisely how he will ascend to the leadership of an overly-rigid military hierarchy in the human resistance does not propel us towards action so much as cautiously step in its direction, weapon raised, speaking into a headset, seeking direction from command. In this, it is also an apt exemplar of the sensibility of the period.

The most interesting element of *Terminator: Salvation* is the brief cameo given to the original film's villain, the T-800. This is achieved not through the use of Arnold Schwarzenegger the actor, but Arnold Schwarzenegger the computer graphic. The T-800 has Schwarzenegger's face, his licensed image grafted digitally onto a younger, fitter extra (Roland Kickinger). Free from the constraint of an actor's bodily presence, Schwarzenegger is evoked only as icon. He is a more threatening figure in this capacity than the sight of his actual body, walking slightly stiffly and delivering awkward one-liners in *The Expendables*. What is significant here is the erasure and refiguration of the presence of 'Arnold Schwarzenegger'. Like the process which allowed Brandon Lee to 'complete' *The Crow* (1994) after his death on set, this is the result of a technical process, but its meaning is far reaching. It calls to mind both Darley's (1997) and Brown's (2009) dire warnings about the indistinguishability of the false and the real, not as a matter of transparent theme as in *The Matrix* but as a matter of practice. This is a far more literal 'rejuvenation' than any of the films featuring 1980s action icons as their older selves, and puts an entirely new complexion on the question of ideological erasure as remarked on by Gary Indiana (2005) and Frank Grady (2003) in the previous chapter.

In many ways precisely the opposite is in play in *Gran Torino* (2008): Clint Eastwood's elegiac swansong as and to the role of action hero. Though Eastwood's comparatively flexible attitude towards his own self-image is evident from as early in his career as *The Gauntlet* (1977) which parodied the gun fetishism of the *Dirty Harry* series, and through films including *Bronco Billy* (1980) and *White Hunter, Black Heart* (1990) where he cast himself against type, he became visibly reflective about age as early as *Unforgiven* (1992) and *In the Line of Fire* (1993), as he began to play 'older' characters sensing increasing disconnection between themselves and the world they now lived in. He thoroughly endorsed the regenerative paradigm of 'the return' as director and star of *Space Cowboys* (2000), which, like *Die Hard 4.0*, plays upon the opposition between machismo and technology. In it a team of elderly test pilots go into space to deal with a satellite guidance system one of them designed. When self-serving beaurocrat Bob Gerson (James Cromwell) tries to pursuade the aged Frank Corvin (Eastwood) to leave the job to younger men, Corvin responds 'The clock is ticking, and I'm only getting older.'

In *Gran Torino* Eastwood presents a sombre and elegaic meditation on his own cinematic image through the prism of the car culture that had also experienced a return in films such as *Taxi* (1998), *Gone in 60 Seconds*

(2000), *The Fast and the Furious* (2001), *The Transporter* and *Death Race* (2008), several of them remakes, most with sequels. In all of these, the motorised vehicle is configured in psychoanalytically fetishistic terms commensurate with John Orr's 'commodified demon' (1993: 127) as discussed in chapter one. In Eastwood's hands, the car reassumes genuine cultural resonance with a consciously ideologically loaded placement of the context of its production and ownership relative to motifs of masculinity and American identity.

Walt Kowalski (Eastwood) is a curmudgeonly Korean War veteran and auto worker whose wife has recently died. Facing old age alone in a neighbourhood increasingly populated by Asian immigrants, he confronts his sense of national identity in the light of the changing complexion of contemporary America. When Thao Van Lor (Bee Vang), a teenage immigrant, attempts to steal his vintage 1972 Ford Gran Torino, which he partly built himself on the construction line in Detriot, Walt finds out that the attempted theft was part of an initiation rite into an Asian street gang. The rites of passage and manhood, it seems, have changed from blue-collar industry to acts of social mischief and criminality.

Against his basic wishes, Walt mentors the boy in the rites of traditional American masculinity, teaching him automotive mechanics and construction techniques ('building' skills in every sense). This brings Walt into conflict with the gang, who continue to pressure Thao and his family. Eventually Walt takes the battle directly to them, suggesting a classic rogue cop or vigilante showdown. Against everyone's expectations (including those of the audience) he goes unarmed, however, and in an act of suicidal self-erasure moves to draw his US Army lighter from his coat and draws fatal gunfire. His death results in the convictions of the gang and the liberation of Thao and his family, and in Walt's will, he bequeaths to Thao his Gran Torino.

Gran Torino is by far the most layered of the 'return' films in respect of its sense of its place in cultural history. In something akin to Brecht's terms where 'real innovations attack the roots' (Owczarski 2006: 9), the film redirects the generic energy that comes with its basic structure and iconography, back to its roots. As Bruce Hedlam remarks, 'if Mr Eastwood shoulders some blame for every *Rambo* and *Die Hard* that followed, he should be given credit for looking at a more complicated transaction in the films he directs, one where people's actions are at odds with their beliefs'

New Americans: Clint Eastwood bequeaths manhood to Bee Vang in *Gran Torino* (2008)

(2008). He notes that what makes this work in *Gran Torino* is the physical presence of Eastwood himself, which though 'iconic' is also tangible. He notes that following the scene in which Walt beats up one of the gang, he returns to his house breathing heavily, exhausted, registering his age, and we believe it. Eastwood as actor, director and symbol of the cinema bids goodbye to the hard-edged traditional American hero, both with affection and a sense of not undue finality.

Eastwood repositions the vigilante film as an intra-social morality tale simply by genuinely surrendering his character's act of will to a broader social process seen to operate as a consequence of but not directly through his decision to intervene – he sees 'justice done' but by an act of suicide: a surrender to death, which is, as we have seen, the real nemesis of every action hero. In drawing correlations between the perceived 'other' world of the encroaching immigrants and his own (embodied by the equally crotchety elderly matriarch of the family next door who grumbles at him as much as he at her, neither understanding the other's language but both understanding the sentiment), the film is able to probe the ideology of difference, and re-locate its sense of moral grounding in the rites of masculinity and car maintenance. As Hedlam observes, Walt's ultimate actions – suicide, self-erasure, and even the disinheritance of his children in favour of Thao – demonstrate an intriguing contradiction not usually permissible in the action hero. The gesture of sacrifice has meaning here. The negating impulse actually represents destruction of a seemingly rigid ideological framework and enables the evolution of a new sense of national identity based on outward growth from immigrant communities.

This is a true return to 'foundational principles' of American democracy in which action becomes both progressive and affirmative entirely apt for millennial America. It is a reaction against reactionism, an unexpected but inevitable dramatisation of the necessity to innovate by attacking the roots, a real 'reboot' which suggests a genuinely new beginning. In a sense it gives promise to the call for an end to the 'murderous ideologies' of the twentieth century without denying the virtues of an ethic of action or the qualities of heroism embodied in an action hero. As a cinematic gesture from one of the icons of the cinema of action, it is poignant, fitting and liberating.

FILMOGRAPHY

Air Force One (Wolfgang Petersen, 1997, US)
Aliens (James Cameron, 1986, US)
American Ninja (Sam Firstenberg, 1985, US)
Armageddon (Michael Bay, 1998, US)
The Assassin (John Badham, 1993, US)
The A-Team (Joe Carnahan, 2010, US)
Bad Boys (Michael Bay, 1995, US)
Bad Boys II (Michael Bay, 2003, US)
Barb Wire (David Hogan, 1996, US)
Beverly Hills Cop (Martin Brest, 1984, US)
Billy Jack (Tom Laughlin, 1971, US)
Billy Jack Goes to Washington (Tom Laughlin, 1977, US)
Black Sunday (John Frankenheimer, 1977, US)
Blazing Saddles (Mel Brooks, 1974, US)
Bloodsport (Newt Arnold, 1988, US)
The Blues Brothers (John Landis, 1980, US)
Blue Steel (Kathryn Bigelow, 1989, US)
Bonnie and Clyde (Arthur Penn, 1967, US)
The Born Losers (Tom Laughlin, 1967, US)
The Bourne Identity (Doug Liman, 2002, US/Germany/Czech Republic)
The Bourne Legacy (Tony Gilroy, 2012, US)
The Bourne Supremacy (Paul Greengrass, 2004, US/Germany)
The Brave One (Neil Jordan, 2007, US)
Bronco Billy (Clint Eastwood, 1980, US)

Brazil (Terry Gilliam, 1985, UK)
Breaker! Breaker! (Don Hulette, 1977, US)
A Bridge Too Far (Richard Attenborough, 1977, UK)
Bullitt (Peter Yates, 1968, US)
Cannonball (Paul Bartel, 1976, US)
The Cannonball Run (Hal Needham, 1981, US)
Casino Royale (Martin Campbell, 2006, US/UK/Germany/Czech Republic)
Charlie's Angels (TV, ABC, 1976–81, US)
Charlie's Angels (McG, 2000, US)
China O'Brien (Robert Clouse, 1990, US)
Cobra (George P. Cosmatos, 1986, US)
Colombiana (Olivier Megaton, 2011, France)
Commando (Mark L. Lester, 1985, US)
Con-Air (Simon West, 1996, US)
Coogan's Bluff (Don Siegel, 1968, US)
The Cosby Show (TV, NBC, 1984–92, US)
Crank (Mark Neveldine, Brian Taylor, 2006, US)
Cross of Iron (Sam Peckinpah, 1977, UK)
The Crow (Alex Proyas, 1994, US)
Damnation Alley (Jack Smight, 1977, US)
Dante's Peak (Roger Donaldson, 1997, US)
The Dark of the Sun (Jack Cardiff, 1968, UK)
Days of Thunder (Tony Scott, 1990, US)
Death Race 2000 (Paul Bartel, 1975, US)
Death Race (Paul W. S. Anderson, 2008, US/Germany/UK)
Death Sentence (James Wan, 2007, US)
Death Wish (Michael Winner, 1974, US)
The Deer Hunter (Michael Cimino, 1978, US)
The Defiant Ones (Stanley Krämer, 1958, US)
Déjà vu (Tony Scott, 2006, US/UK)
Deliverance (John Boorman, 1972, US)
The Delta Force (Menahem Golan, 1986, US)
Demolition Man (Marco Brambilla, 1993, US)
The Detective (Gordon Douglas, 1968, US)
Die Another Day (Lee Tamahori, 2002, US/UK)
Die Hard (John McTiernan, 1988, US)
Die Hard 2 (Renny Harlin, 1990, US)

Die Hard With a Vengeance (John McTiernan, 1995, US)

Die Hard 4.0 (Len Wiseman, 2007, US)

Dip huet seung hung (*The Killer*) (John Woo, 1989, Hong Kong)

Dirty Harry (Don Siegel, 1971, US)

The Driver (Walter Hill, 1978, US)

Dog Day Afternoon (Sidney Lumet, 1975, US)

The Dogs of War (John Irvin, 1980, UK)

Domino (Tony Scott, 2005, US/France)

Double Team (Tsui Hark, 1997, US)

Dredd 3D (Pete Travis, 2012, US/UK/India)

The Driver (Walter Hill, 1978, US)

Duel (Steven Spielberg, 1971, US)

Eraser (Chuck Russell, 1996, US)

Enter the Dragon (Robert Clouse, 1973, US/Hong Kong)

Eve of Destruction (Duncan Gibbons, 1991, US)

Executive Decision (Stuart Baird, 1996, US)

The Expendables (Sylvester Stallone, 2010, US)

The Expendables 2 (Simon West, 2012, US)

An Eye for an Eye (Steve Carver, 1981, US)

Face/Off (John Woo, 1997, US)

The Fast and the Furious (Rob Cohen, 2001, US)

First Blood (Ted Kotcheff, 1982, US)

48 Hrs. (Walter Hill, 1982, US)

The French Connection (William Friedkin, 1971, US)

Gator (Burt Reynolds, 1976, US)

The Gauntlet (Clint Eastwood, 1977, US)

G.I. Jane (Ridley Scott, 1997, US)

Gone in 60 Seconds (H. B. Halicki, 1974, US)

Gone in 60 Seconds (Dominic Sena, 2000, US)

Gran Torino (Clint Eastwood, 2008, US)

The Green Berets (John Wayne, 1968, US)

The Gumball Rally (Charles Ball, 1976, US)

Hanna (Joe Wright, 2011, US/UK/Germany)

Hard Target (John Woo, 1994, US)

The Hard Way (John Badham, 1991, US)

Harry Potter and the Philosopher's Stone (Chris Columbus, 2001, US/UK)

Haywire (Steven Soderbergh, 2011, US/Ireland)

High Noon (Fred Zinneman, 1952, US)

Hickey & Boggs (Robert Culp, 1972, US)

A History of Violence (David Cronenberg, 2005, US/Germany)

Hostel (Eli Roth, 2005, US)

Hot Fuzz (Edgar Wright, 2007, UK/France/US)

Hot Shots! Part Deux (Jim Abrahams, 1993, US)

Hung fan au (*Rumble in the Bronx*, 1995, Hong Kong)

The Hurt Locker (Kathryn Bigelow, 2008, US)

Independence Day (Roland Emmerich, 1996, US)

In the Heat of the Night (Norman Jewison, 1967, US)

In the Line of Fire (Wolfgang Petersen, 1993, US)

Invasion USA (Joseph Zito, 1985, US)

I Spy (TV, NBC, 1965-68, US)

Jarhead (Sam Mendes, 2005, US)

JCVD (Mabrouk El Mechri, 2008, Belgium/Luxembourg/France)

Jing wu men (*Fist of Fury*) (Lo Wei, 1972, Hong Kong)

Jing wu ying xiong (*Fist of Legend*) (Gordon Chan, 1994, Hong Kong)

Judge Dredd (Danny Cannon, 1995, US)

The Junkman: Gone in 60 Seconds II (H. B. Halicki, 1982, US)

Jurassic Park (Steven Spielberg, 1993, US)

Kickboxer (Mark DiSalle, David Worth, 1989, US)

Kill Bill Vol. 1 (Quentin Tarantino, 2003, US)

Kill Bill Vol. 2 (Quentin Tarantino, 2004, US)

Kick-Ass (Matthew Vaughn, 2010, US/UK)

Kung-Fu (TV, Warner Bros. Television,1972–75, US)

Last Action Hero (John McTiernan, 1993, US)

Lara Croft: Tomb Raider (Simon West, 2001, US)

Lat sau san taam (*Hard Boiled*) (John Woo, 1992, Hong Kong)

The Last Boy Scout (Tony Scott, 1991, US)

Licence to Kill (John Glen, 1989, US/UK)

Léon (Luc Besson, 1994, France)

Lethal Weapon(Richard Donner, 1987, US)

Lethal Weapon 2 (Richard Donner, 1989, US)

Lethal Weapon 3 (Richard Donner, 1992, US)

Lethal Weapon 4 (Richard Donner, 1998, US)

Lock, Stock, and Two Smoking Barrels (Guy Ritchie, 1998, UK)

Lone Wolf McQuade (Steve Carver, 1982, US)

The Lost World: Jurassic Park (Steven Spielberg, 1997, US)
The Long Kiss Goodnight (Renny Harlin, 1996, US)
The Long Riders (Walter Hill, 1980, US)
The Lord of the Rings: The Fellowship of the Ring (Peter Jackson, 2001,
    New Zealand/US)
Madigan (Don Siegel, 1968, US)
Mad Max (George Miller, 1979, Australia)
Mad Max 2 (George Miller, 1981, Australia)
Mad Max Beyond Thunderdome (George Miller, George Ogilvie 1985,
    Australia)
The Magnificent Seven (John Sturges, 1960, US)
The Manchurian Candidate (Jonathan Demme, 2004, US)
Man on Fire (Tony Scott, 2004, US/UK)
The Matrix (Andy Wachowski, Larry Wachowski, 1999, US)
The Matrix Reloaded (Andy Wachowski, Larry Wachowski, 2003, US)
The Matrix Revolutions (Andy Wachowski, Larry Wachowski, 2003, US)
Maximum Risk (Ringo Lam, 1996, US)
The Mechanic (Michael Winner, 1972, US)
The Mechanic (Simon West, 2011, US)
The Mechanik (Dolph Lundgren, 2005, US/Germany)
Meng long guo jiang (The Way of the Dragon) (Bruce Lee, 1972, Hong
    Kong)
Missing in Action (Joseph Zito, 1984, US)
Missionary Man (Dolph Lundgren, 2007, US)
Mr. and Mrs. Smith (Doug Liman, 2005, US)
Munich (Steven Spielberg, 2005, US)
National Lampoon's Loaded Weapon 1 (Gene Quintano, 1993, US)
Natural Born Killers (Oliver Stone, 1994, US)
Nico (Andrew Davis, 1988, US)
Nighthawks (Bruce Malmuth, 1981, US)
Nikita (Luc Besson, 1990, France)
No Retreat, No Surrender (Corey Yuen, 1986, US)
Once Upon a Time in China (Tsui Hark, 1991, Hong Kong)
The One (James Wong, 2001, US)
On Her Majesty's Secret Service (Peter Hunt, 1969, UK)
Out for Justice (John Flynn, 1991, US)
Outlaw (Nick Love, 2007, UK)

Passenger 57 (Kevin Hooks, 1992, US)
Patton (Franklin J. Schaffner, 1970, US)
Point Break (Kathryn Bigelow, 1991, US)
Point Blank (John Boorman, 1967, US)
Predator (John McTiernan, 1987, US)
The Professionals (Richard Brooks, 1966, US)
Pumping Iron (George Butler, 1977, US)
The Punisher (Mark Goldblatt, 1989, US/Australia)
The Punisher (Jonathan Hensleigh, 2004, US/Germany)
Punisher: War Zone (Lexi Alexander, 2008, US/Germany/Canada)
Raiders of the Lost Ark (Steven Spielberg, 1981, US)
Raid on Entebee (Irvin Kershner, 1976, US)
Rambo (Sylvester Stallone, 2008, US)
Rambo: First Blood Part II (George P. Cosmatos, 1985, US)
Rambo III (Peter MacDonald, 1988, US)
RED (Robert Schwentke, 2010, US)
Red Dawn (John Milius, 1984, US)
Red Dawn (Dan Bradley, 2012, US)
Replicant (Ringo Lam, 2001, US)
Road House (Rowdy Herrington, 1989, US)
Robocop (Paul Verhoeven, 1987, US)
Robocop (José Padilha, 2013, US)
Robocop 2 (Irvin Kershner, 1990, US)
The Rock (Michael Bay, 1995, US)
Rocky (John G. Avildsen, 1976, US)
Rocky Balboa (Sylvester Stallone, 2006, US)
The Running Man (Paul Michael Glaser, 1987, US)
Rush Hour (Brett Ratner, 1998, US)
Salt (Philip Noyce, 2010, US)
Saving Private Ryan (Steven Spielberg, 1998, US)
Saw (James Wan, 2004, US)
The Seventh Seal (Ingmar Bergman, 1957, Sweden)
The Seven-Ups (Philip D'Antoni, 1973, US)
Shanghai Noon (Tom Dey, 2000, US)
Shanghai Knights (David Dobkin, 2003, US)
The Siege (Edward Zwick, 1998, US)
Smokey and the Bandit (Hal Needham, 1977, US)

Snatch (Guy Ritchie, 2000, US/UK)
Southern Comfort (Walter Hill, 1981, US)
Space Cowboys (Clint Eastwood, 2000, US)
Speed (Jan de Bont, 1994, US)
Star Wars Episode I: The Phantom Menace (George Lucas, 1999, US)
Stay Hungry (Bob Rafelson, 1976, US)
Straw Dogs (Sam Peckinpah, 1971, UK)
Straw Dogs (Rod Lurie, 2011, US)
Tango & Cash (Andrey Konchalovsky, 1989, US)
Taken (Pierre Morel, 2008, France)
Taken 2 (Olivier Megaton, 2012, France)
Taxi (Gerard Pires, 1998, France)
Taxi Driver (Martin Scorsese, 1976, US)
The Terminator (James Cameron, 1984, US)
Terminator 2: Judgment Day (James Cameron, 1991, US)
Terminator 3: Rise of the Machines (Jonathan Mostow, 2003, US)
Terminator Salvation (McG, 2009, US)
The Transporter (Corey Yuen, 2002, France/US)
Timecop (Peter Hyams, 1994, US)
Titanic (James Cameron, 1997, US)
Top Gun (Tony Scott, 1986, US)
Total Recall (Paul Verhoeven, 1990, US)
Total Recall (Len Wiseman, 2012, US/Canada)
The Trial of Billy Jack (Tom Laughlin, 1974, US)
True Grit (Henry Hathaway, 1969, US)
True Lies (James Cameron, 1994, US)
True Romance (Tony Scott, 1993, US)
The Tuxedo (Kevin Donovan, 2002, US)
Twister (Jan de Bont, 1996, US)
Two-Lane Blacktop (Monte Hellman, 1971, US)
Uncommon Valor (Ted Kotcheff, 1983, US)
Under Siege (Andrew Davis, 1992, US)
Unforgiven (Clint Eastwood, 1992, US)
Universal Soldier (Cy Endfield, 1971, UK)
Universal Soldier (Roland Emmerlich, 1992, US)
Vanishing Point (Richard C. Sarafian, 1971, US)
Victory at Entebee (Marvin J. Chomsky, 1976, US)

Volcano (Mick Jackson, 1997, US)
Walker, Texas Ranger (CBS, 1992–2001, US)
Walking Tall (Phil Karlson, 1973, US)
War (Philip Atwell, 2007, US)
A Warning from Hollywood (Steve Bradshaw, transmission date 24 March
     2002, UK)
The Warriors (Walter Hill, 1979, US)
Week-End (Jean-Luc Goddard, 1967, Fra.)
We Were Soldiers (Randall Wallace, 2002, US)
White Hunter, Black Heart (Clint Eastwood, 1990, US)
White Lightning (Joseph Sergeant, 1973, US)
The Wild Bunch (Sam Peckinpah, 1969, US)
The Wild Geese (Andrew V. McLaglen, 1978, UK)
Wanted (Timur Bekmambetov, 2008 US/Germany)
Wu hu cang long (*Crouching Tiger, Hidden Dragon*) (Ang Lee, 2000,
     Taiwan/US/Hong Kong/China)

BIBLIOGRAPHY

Altman, R. (1999) *Film/Genre*. London: British Film Institute.

Anderson, A. (1998) 'Action in Motion: Kinesthesia in Martial Arts Films', *Jump Cut*, 42, 1–11, 83.

Andrews, N. (1973) 'Sam Peckinpah: the survivor and the individual', *Sight & Sound*, 42, 2, 69–74.

Ballard, K. (2007) 'The Privitisation of Military Affairs: A Historical Look into the Evolution of the Private Military Industry', in T. Jager and G. Kummel (eds) *Private Military and Secruity Companies: Chances, Problems, Pitfalls and Prospects*. Berlin: VS Verlag, 37–53.

Barr, C. (1972) '*Straw Dogs, A Clockwork Orange* and the Critics', *Screen*, 13, 2, 17–31.

Bean, J. (2004) '"Trauma Thrills": Notes on Early Action Cinema', in Y. Tasker (ed.) *Action and Adventure Cinema*. London and New York: Routledge, 17–30.

Best, S. (1989) 'Robocop: In the ditritus of hi-technology', *Jump Cut*, 34, March, 19–26.

Bordwell, D. (2000) *Planet Hong Kong: Popular Cinema and the Art of Entertainment*. Cambridge, Massachusetts, and London, England: Harvard University Press.

____ (2002) 'Intensified Continuity: Visual Style in Contemporary American Film', *Film Quarterly*, 55, 3, 16–28.

____ (2008) *Poetics of Cinema*, New York and London: Routledge.

Brode, D. (1990) *The Films of the Eighties*. New York: Citadel Press.

____ (2003) *Boys and Toys: Ultimate Action Adventure Movies*. New York: Citadel Press.

Broderick, M. (1993) 'Heroic Apocalypse: Mad Max, Mythology and the Millennium', in C. Sharrett (ed.) *Crisis Cinema: The Apocalyptic Idea in Postmodern Narrative Film*. Washington DC: Maisonneuve Press, 250–72.

Brown, W. (2009) 'Man without a movie camera – movies without men: towards a posthumanist cinema?', in W. Buckland (ed.) *Film Theory and Contemporary Hollywood Movies*. New York and London: Routledge, 66–85.

Buckland, W. (2009) (ed.) *Film Theory and Contemporary Hollywood Movies*. New York and London: Routledge.

Buscombe, E. (ed.) (1993) *The British Film Institute Companion to the Western*. New edition. London: British Film Institute.

Bush, G. H. W. (1989) 'Inaugural Address'. On-line. Available at: http://bushlibrary.tamu.edu/research/public_papers.php?id=1&year=1989&month=all (accessed 17 December 2010).

Bush, G. W. (2001) 'President Bush's address to a joint session of Congress on Thursday night, September 20, 2001'. On-line. Available at: http://archives.cnn.com/2001/US/09/20/gen.bush.transcript (accessed 17 December 2010).

Chute, D. (1982) 'The Ayatollah of the Moviola', *Film Comment*, 18, 4, 26–31.

Clarke, G. (1985) 'New Muscle at the Box Office' in *Time Magazine*. On-line. Available at: http://www.time.com/time/magazine/article/0,9171,960242-1,00.html (accessed 17 December 2010).

Coward, R. and J. Ellis (1981) 'Hong Kong – China 1981', *Screen*, 22, 4, 91–100.

Cutts, J. (1969) 'Shoot!', *Films and Filming*, 16, 1, October, 4–8.

Darley, A. (1997) 'Second-order realism and post-modernist aesthetics in computer animation', in J. Pilling (ed.) *A Reader in Animation Studies*. London: John Libbey, 16–24.

Davies, P. and B. Neve (eds) (1981) *Cinema, Politics and Society in America*. Manchester: Manchester University Press.

Dawson, A. (2008) *Studying The Matrix*. Leighton Buzzard: Auteur.

Diawara, M. (ed.) (1993) *Black American Cinema*. New York and London: AFI.

Durgnat, R. (1969) *The Crazy Mirror: Hollywood Comedy and the American Image*. New York: Delta Books.

Eberwein, R. (ed.) (2002) *The War Film*. New Brunswick, New Jersey and London: Rutgers University Press.

Elsaesser, T. (ed.) (1990) *Early Cinema: Space, Frame Narrative*. London: British Film Institute.

Elsaesser, T. and W. Buckland (2002) *Studying Contemporary American Film: A Guide to Movie Analysis*. London: Hodder Arnold.

Farrell, K. (1998) *Post-traumatic Culture: Injury and Interpretation in the Nineties*. Baltimore: Johns Hopkins University Press.

Ferguson, K. (2008) 'Yuppie devil: villainy in Kathryn Bigelow's *Blue Steel*', *Jump Cut*, 50. On-line. Available at: http://www.ejumpcut.org/archive/jc50.2008/BlueSteel/index.html (accessed 17 December 2010).

Frandley, M. (2004) 'Maximus Melodramaticus: Masculinity, Masochism and White Male Paranoia in Contemporary Hollywood Cinema', in Y. Tasker (ed.) *Action and Adventure Cinema*. London: Routledge, 235–51.

Gallagher, T. (2003) 'Shoot-Out at the Genre Corral: Problems in the "Evolution" of the Western', in B. Grant (ed.) *Film Genre Reader III*. Austin: University of Texas Press, 262–76.

Giroux, H. (2002) *Breaking in to the Movies: Film and the Culture of Politics*. Oxford: Blackwell.

Gough-Yates, A. (2001) 'Angels in Chains?: Feminism, Femininity and Consumer Culture in *Charlie's Angels*', in B. Osgerby and A. Gough-Yates (eds) *Action TV: Tough Guys, Smooth Operators and Foxy Chicks*. London and New York: Routledge, 83–99.

Grady, F. (2003) 'Arnoldian Humanism, or Amensia and Autobiography in the Schwarzenegger Action Film', *Cinema Journal*, 42, 2, 41–56.

Grant, B. K. (ed.) (2003) *Film Genre Reader III*. Austin: University of Texas Press.

____ (2007) *Film Genre: From Iconography to Ideology*. London: Wallflower Press.

Greven, D. (2009) *Manhood in Hollywood: From Bush to Bush*. Austin: University of Texas Press.

Grieveson, L. and P. Krämer (eds) *The Silent Cinema Reader*. London and New York: Routledge.

Guerrero, E. (1993) 'The Black Image in Protective Custody: Hollywood's Biracial Buddy Films of the Eighties', in M. Diawara (ed.) *Black American Cinema*. New York: American Film Institute, 237–46.

Hampton, H. (2005) 'Extreme Prejudice: Transgressive cinema from Anthony Mann's prototypical *The Furies* to the terminal postmodernism of *Kill Bill* and *Sin City*', *Film Comment*, 41, 6, 50–5.

Harman, C. (2008) '1968: The Year the World Caught Fire', *Socialist Review*, 325, May, 10–12, 14, 16.

Haraway, D. (1991) *Simians, Cyborgs and Women: The Reinvention of Nature*. New York: Routledge.

Hedlam, B. (2008) 'The Films Are for Him: Got That?', in *The New York Times*, 10 December 2008. On-line. Available at: http://www.nytimes.com/2008/12/14/movies/14head.html?_r=1&pagewanted=2 (accessed 17 December 2010).

Hicks, N. (2002) *Writing the Action-Adventure Film: The Moment of Truth*. Studio City, CA: Michael Wiese Productions.

Hills, E. (1999) 'From "figurative males" to action heroines: further thoughts on active women in the cinema', *Screen*, 40, 1, Spring, 38–50.

Hill, J. and P. Church Gibson (eds) (1998) *The Oxford Guide to Film Studies*. Oxford and New York: Oxford University Press.

Higgins, S. (2008) 'Suspenseful Situations: Melodramatic Narrative and Contemporary Action Film', *Cinema Journal*, 47, 2, 74–96.

Hoberman, J. (2005) 'The Servant', *Film Comment*, 41, 3, May–June, 28–34.

Holmlund, C. (2004) 'Europeans in Action!', in Y. Tasker (ed.) *Action and Adventure Cinema*. London and New York: Routledge, 284–96.

Hunt, L. (2004) 'The Hong Kong/Hollywood Connection: Stardom and Spectacle in Trasnational Action Cinema', in Y. Tasker (ed.) *Action and Adventure Cinema*. London and New York: Routledge, 270–83.

Hutchings, P. (1993) 'Masculinity and the Horror Film', in P. Kirtzham and J. Thumin (eds) *You Tarzan: Masculinity, Movies and Men*. London: Lawrence & Wishart, 84–94.

Indiana, G. (2005) *Schwarzenegger Syndrome: Politics and Celebrity in the Age of Contempt*. New York and London: The New Press.

Jäger, T. and G. Kümmel (eds) (2007) *Private Military and Security Companies: Chances, Problems, Pitfalls and Prospects*. Berlin: VS Verlag.

Jacoby, S. (2008) *The Age of American Unreason*. New York: Pantheon.

Jeffords, S. (1994) *Hard Bodies: Hollywood Masculinity in the Reagan Era*. New Brunswick, NJ: Rutgers University Press.

Johnson, D. (1981) 'Vigilance and the Law: The Moral Authority of

Popular Justice in the Far West', *American Quarterly*, 33, 5, 558–86.

Kael, P. (1985) *5001 Nights at the Movies*, Austin, TX: Holt, Rinehart and Winston/Owl Books.

Keane, S. (2006) *Disaster Movies: The Cinema of Catastrophe*. Revised edition. London: Wallflower Press.

King, N. (1999) *Heroes in Hard Times: Cop Action Movies in the US*. Philadelphia: Temple University Press.

Kinsey, C. (2007) 'Private Security Companies: Agents of Democracy or Simply Mercenaries?', in T. Jäger and G. Kümmel (eds) *Private Military and Security Companies: Chances, Problems, Pitfalls and Prospects*. Berlin: VS Verlag, 87–194.

Kirtzham, P. and J. Thumin (1993) (eds) *You Tarzan: Masculinity, Movies and Men*. London: Lawrence & Wishart.

Krämer, P. (1998) 'Post-classical Hollywood', in J. Hill and P. Church Gibson (eds) *The Oxford Guide to Film Studies*. Oxford and New York: Oxford University Press, 289–309.

Knapp, L. (2008) 'Tony Scott and Domino – Say hello (and goodbye) to the postclassical', in *Jump Cut*, 50. On-line. Available at: http://www.ejumpcut.org/archive/jc50.2008/DominoKnapp/index.html (accessed 17 December 2010).

Kolker, R. (1980) *A Cinema of Loneliness*. New York and Oxford: Oxford University Press.

Krämer, P. (2005) *The New Hollywood: From Bonnie and Clyde to Star Wars*. London and New York: Wallflower Press.

Lichtenfeld, E. (2007) *Action Speaks Louder: Violence, Spectacle, and The American Action Movie*. Middletown, CT: Wesleyan University Press.

Logan, B. (1996) *Hong Kong Action Cinema*. Woodstock, NY: The Overlook Press.

Lovell, A. (1975) *Don Siegel*. London: British Film Institute.

McCaughey, M. and N. King (2001) *Reel Knockouts: Violent Women in the Movies*. Austin: University of Texas Press.

Mercer, J. and M. Shingler (2004) *Melodrama: Genre, Style, Sensibility*. London and New York: Wallflower Press.

Monaco, J. (1979) *American Film Now*. New York, London and Scarborough, Ontario: New American Library.

Moncao, P. (2001) *The Sixties: 1960–1969*. Berkeley, CA: University of California Press.

Neale, S. (1980) *Genre*. London: British Film Institute.

____ (2003) 'Questions of Genre', in B. Grant (ed.) *Film Genre Reader III*. Austin: University of Texas Press, 160–84.

Nietzsche, F. (2003 [1886]) *Beyond Good and Evil*. Trans. R. Hollingdale. London and New York: Penguin.

Newman, K. (2000) *Apocalypse Movies: End of the World Cinema*. New York: St. Martin's Press.

Norris, C. (2003) 'Mixed Blood', in *Film Comment*, 39, 6, Nov./Dec., 26–8.

____ (2008) *Black Belt Patriotism: How to Reawaken America*. Washington, DC: Regenery Publishing Inc.

O'Brien, G. (2003) 'Devotional Furies', *Film Comment*, 39, 6, 22–5.

O'Brien, H. (2002) 'Millennial Mindgames', *Film and Film Culture*, 2002, 1, 105–14.

O'Day, M. (2004) 'Beauty in Motion: Gender, Spectacle and Action Babe Cinema', in Y. Tasker (ed.) *Action and Adventure Cinema*. London and New York: Routledge, 201–18.

Orr, J. (1993) *Cinema and Modernity*. Oxford: Polity Press.

Osgerby, B. and A. Gough-Yates (eds) (2001) *Action TV: Tough Guys, Smooth Operators and Foxy Chicks*. London and New York: Routledge.

Parish, J. R. (2006) *Fiasco: A History of Hollywood's Iconic Flops*. Hoboken, NJ: John Wiley & Sons.

Owczarski, K. (2006) 'Articulating the Violence Debate', *Cineaction*, 68, 2–10.

Pfeil, F. (1995) *White Guys: Studies in Postodern Domination and Difference*. London: Verso.

Pilling, J. (ed.) (1997) *A Reader in Animation Studies*. London, Paris, Rome, Sydney: John Libbey.

Polan, D. (2002) 'Auteurism and War-teurism: Terrence Malick's War Movie', in R. Eberwein (ed.) *The War Film*. New Brunswick, NJ: Rutgers University Press, 53–61.

Popple, S. and J. Kember (2004) *Early Cinema: From Factory Gate to Dream Factory*. London: Wallflower Press.

Prince, S. (2003) *Classical Film Violence*. New Brunswick, NJ: Rutgers University Press.

____ (2007) 'Introduction?' in S. Prince (ed.) *American Cinema of the 1980s*. New Brunswick, NJ: Rutgers University Press, 1–21.

____ (2009) *Firestorm: American Film in the Age of Terrorism*. New York:

Columbia University Press.

Rayns, T. (1974) 'Threads Through the Laybrinth: Hong Kong Movies', *Sight & Sound*, 43, 3, 138–41.

Reynolds, D. (2009) *America, Empire of Liberty: A New History*. London: Allen Lane.

Robinson, C. (1998) 'Blaxploitation and the misrepresentation of liberation', *Race & Class*, 40, 1, 1–12.

Rodriguez, H. (1997) 'Hong Kong popular culture as an interpretive arena: the Huang Feihong film series', *Screen*, 38, 1, 1–24.

Romao, T. (2004) 'Guns and Gas: Investigating the 1970s car chase film', in Y. Tasker (ed.) *Action and Adventure Cinema*. London and New York: Routledge, 130–52.

Romney, J. (1993) 'Arnold Through the Looking Glass', *Sight & Sound*, 3, 8, 7–9.

Sanders, J. (2009) *Studying Disaster Movies*. Leighton Buzzard: Auteur.

Sardar, Z. and M. W. Davies (2004) *American Dream: Global Nightmare*. Cambridge: Icon Books.

Schatz, T. (2009) 'New Hollywood, New Millenium', in W. Buckland (ed.) *Film Theory and Contemporary Hollywood Movies*. New York and London: Routledge, 19–46.

Schickel, R. (1985) 'Danger: Live Moral Issues', in *Time Magazine*. On-line. Available at: http://www.time.com/time/magazine/article/0,9171,957002,00.html (accessed 17 December 2010).

Schopenhauer, A. (1958 [1844]) *The World as Will and Representation*. Trans. E. Payne. New York: Dover Publications.

Schneider, S. (ed.) (2010) *101 Action Movies You Must See Before You Die*. London: Quintessence.

Scott, A. (2008) 'It's All About Him, No Matter Who He Claims to Be', in *The New York Times*, 7 November 2008. On-line. Available at: http://movies.nytimes.com/2008/11/07/movies/07jcvd.html (accessed 17 December 2010).

Semmerling, T. J. (2006) *'Evil' Arabs in American Popular Film*. Austin: University of Texas Press.

Shaffer, L. (1972) '*The Wild Bunch* versus *Straw Dogs*', *Sight & Sound*, 41, 3, 132–3.

Sharrett, C. (1993) *Crisis Cinema: The Apocalyptic Idea in Postmodern Narrative Film*. Washington, DC: Maisonneuve Press.

Stallone, S. (2008) 'Interview', *Uncut,* 131, April, 18.

Stout, R. (2005) *Action*. Chesham: Acumen.

Strauven, W. (ed.) (2006) *The Cinema of Attractions Reloaded*. Amsterdam: Amsterdam University Press.

Stringer, J. (1997) '"Your tender smiles give me strength": paradigms of masculinity in John Woo's *A Better Tomorrow* and *The Killer*', *Screen*, 38, 1, 25–41.

Studlar, G. and D. Desser (1988) 'Never Having to Say You're Sorry: *Rambo*'s Rewriting of the Vietnam War', *Film Quarterly*, 42, 1, 9–16.

Sturken, M. (1997) *Tangled Memories: The Vietnam War, the AIDS Epidemic, and the Politics of Remembering*. Berkeley, CA: University of California Press.

Suid, L. (2002) *Guts & Glory: The Making of the American Military Image in Film*. Second edition. Lexington, KY: University Press of Kentucky.

Talbot, P. (2006) *Bronson's Loose!: The Making of the Death Wish Films*. New York, Lincoln and Shanghai: iUniverse.

Tasker, Y. (1993) *Spectacular Bodies: Gender, Genre and the Action Cinema*. London: Routledge.

____ (2004) 'Introduction?' in Y. Tasker (ed.) *Action and Adventure Cinema*. London: Routledge, 1–13.

Teo, S. (1997) *Hong Kong Cinema: The Extra Dimensions*. London: British Film Institute.

Thorp, R. (1979) *Nothing Lasts Forever*. London, New York, Victoria, Ontario, Auckland: Penguin.

Tomasovic, D. (2006) 'The Hollywood Cobweb: New Laws of Attraction', in W. Strauven (ed.) *The Cinema of Attractions Reloaded*. Amsterdam: Amsterdam University Press, 309–20.

Traister, R., E. Franck and I. Belcher (2001) 'Oliver Stone and Christopher Hitchens Spar Over Hollywood's Efforts to be Relevant', in *The New York Observer*, 14 October. On-line. Available at: http://www. observer.com/2001/oliver-stone-and-christopher-hitchens-spar-over-hollywoods-efforts-be-relevant (accessed 17 December 2010).

Vitali, V. (2010) *Hindi Action Cinema: Industires, Narratives, Bodies*. Bloomington, IN: Indiana University Press.

Von Doviak, S. (2005) *Hick Flicks: The Rise and Fall of Rednick Cinema*. Jefferson, NC: McFarland.

Walker, B. (1971) 'Two-Lane Blacktop', *Sight & Sound*, 40, 1, 34–7.

Wartenberg, T. (2005) 'Philosophy Screened: Experiencing *The Matrix*', in T. Wartenberg and A. Curran (eds) *The Philosophy of Film*. Oxford: Blackwell, 270–83.

Wartenberg , T and A. Curran (eds) (2005) *The Philosophy of Film*. Malden, Oxford, Victoria: Blackwell Publishing.

West, D. (2006) *Chasing Dragons: An Introduction to the Martial Arts Film*. London and New York: IB Tauris.

Westerbeck, C. (1976) 'Beauties and the Beast', *Sight & Sound*, 45, 3, Summer, 134–9.

Westwell, G. (2006) *War Cinema: Hollywood on the Front Line*. London: Wallflower Press.

Williams, L. (1991) 'Film Bodies: Gender, Genre, and Excess', *Film Quarterly*, 4, 44, 2–13.

Williams, T. (2000) 'Under "Western Eyes": The Personal Odyssey of Huang Fei-Hong in *Once Upon a Time in China*', *Cinema Journal*, 40, 2, 3–24.

Wright, W. (1975) *Sixguns & Society*. Berkeley, CA: University of California Press.

Žižek, S. (2006) *The Parallax View*. Cambridge, MA: MIT Press.

____ (2008) *Violence: Six Sideways Reflections*. London: Profile.

____ (2010) *Living in the End Times*. London: Verso.

Zoglin, R. (1985) 'An Outbreak of Rambomania', in *Time Magazine*. On-line. Available at: http://www.time.com/time/magazine/article/0,9171,142090,00.html (accessed 17 December 2010).

INDEX

comedy 51, 63, 82
community 26, 28, 30, 50
Coward, Rosalind 77
Cox, Ronny 60
Craig, Daniel 91
crime 1, 12, 20, 22–3, 28, 35, 49,
	56
culture wars 4
cyborg 58–9, 66, 82

Darley, Andy 82–3, 107
Dawson, Anna 85
democracy 94, 96, 110
Desser, David 6
digital 15, 76, 80, 83, 99–100,
	104, 107
disaster 16, 30, 40, 59, 73, 76
Dudikoff, Michael 45, 49
Durgnat, Raymond 63–5

Eastwood, Clint 16, 20–2, 45,
	107–9
Egendorf, Arthur 7
Eisenstein, Sergei 74
Ellis, John 77
El Mechri, Mabrouk 101
Elsaesser, Thomas 33, 70, 97

fantasy 3, 7–8, 15–16, 20, 28, 34,
	61, 71, 85, 92, 102, 105
Farrell, Kirby 42–5
fascist 22–3, 75
feminist 66–7
Ferguson, Kevin 66
Ford, Harrison 5
Frandley, Martin 57
frontier 18, 23–4, 40, 79

Freud, Sigmund 64

Gance, Abel 74
Gibson, Mel 37–8, 45, 53
Giroux, Henri 94
Glover, Danny 53
Gough-Yates, Anna 67–8
government 19, 24, 31, 46, 49, 61,
	87–8, 92
Grady, Frank 84–5, 107
Grant, Barry Keith 5
Greven, David 71
Guerrero, Ed 51
Gulf War Syndrome 69

Hackman, Gene 22
Hamilton, Linda 58–9
Hampton, Howard 94
Haraway, Donna 59
homoerotic 64, 71
homophobia 68
homosexual 21, 64–5, 101
humour 51, 57–8, 62–5, 80
Hapkido 25
Hamlet 1, 7, 17
healing 58–9
Hedlam, Bruce 108–9
Hellman, Monte 37
hero 1, 3, 12, 14, 16, 19, 35, 40,
	45, 47, 52, 54–6, 61, 67, 69,
	71–3, 86, 93, 102–3
Hicks, Neill 28
Hill, Walter 51
Holmlund, Christine 81
Hong Kong 9–10, 15, 25, 77–8,
	84, 98
Hunt, Leon 80